D1607612

NATHAN
BEDFORD
FORREST'S
REDEMPTION

Nathan Bedford Forrest's Redemption

Shane E. Kastler

PELICAN PUBLISHING COMPANY
Gretna 2010

*The word "Pelican" and the depiction of a pelican
are trademarks of Pelican Publishing Company, Inc.,
and are registered in the U.S. Patent and Trademark Office.*

Library of Congress Cataloging-in-Publication Data

Kastler, Shane E.
  Nathan Bedford Forrest's redemption / Shane E. Kastler.
    p. cm.
  Includes bibliographical references and index.
  ISBN 978-1-58980-834-8 (hardcover : alk. paper) 1. Forrest, Nathan
Bedford, 1821-1877. 2. Forrest, Nathan Bedford, 1821-1877—Religion.
3. Generals—Confederate States of America—Biography. 4. Confederate
States of America. Army—Biography. I. Title.
  E467.1.F72K37 2010
  355.0092—dc22
  [B]
                    2010020290

When denoted "KJV", Scripture taken from the KING JAMES VERSION
of the Bible, also known as the "Authorized Version" (AV).

When denoted "NASB", Scripture taken from the NEW AMERICAN
STANDARD BIBLE®, copyright © 1960, 1962, 1963, 1968, 1971,
1972, 1973, 1975, 1977, 1995 by The Lockman Foundation. Used by
permission.

Printed in the United States of America
Published by Pelican Publishing Company, Inc.
1000 Burmaster Street, Gretna, Louisiana 70053

To my wife, Erin

As General Forrest had Mary Ann, so I have you,
a faithful Christian encourager to help navigate the storms of life.

Contents

Acknowledgments

Many people should be thanked for the production of this book. I would first like to extend my gratitude to all historians and Forrest biographers, both alive and deceased, who came before me. In many ways I stand on their shoulders and am grateful for their hard work and research into Forrest's life. Among these are John Wyeth, Robert Selph Henry, Andrew Nelson Lytle, Jack Hurst, Brian Steel Willis, Edwin Bearss, Eddy W. Davison, Daniel Foxx, Michael R. Bradley, and Shelby Foote.

In no particular order I would also like to thank the following people. The congregation of the First Christian Church of Pleasanton, Kansas, a warm and accepting nondenominational church, graciously welcomed and supported an outspoken Southern Baptist pastor for five years. I thank them from the bottom of my heart. Mary Jane Heiser and Sue Jackson, fellow-workers of the church, always kept me company and provided needed breaks from the monotony of writing while offering constant encouragement in my endeavors. From my parents, Charles and Norma Kastler, as well as my wife's parents, Jack and Jackie Selph, I have received nothing but encouragement and support for anything I've attempted to do, and I am grateful. I also thank my father-in-law, Jack, and my wife, Erin, for proofreading my initial manuscript and offering many helpful suggestions. Other family members whose kind words of encouragement have been invaluable include: Kevin and Julie Kastler, Michael and Kimberly Gelsthorpe, Casey and Kayla Selph, Robbie and Denisa Selph, Bill and Sandy Johnson, and Loretta Selph.

My wife, Erin, has spent her entire married life offering

9

constant encouragement, prayer, support, and faithfulness to me, willingly and graciously moving around the country, all the while making every house we live in a home. To say she is one in a million would not come close to doing her justice. Indeed, she is one of a kind. I thank her, as well as my three children, Andrew, Savannah, and Karissa, who have endured countless stories around the dinner table about ol' Bedford, Stonewall, Jeb, General Lee, and countless other Confederate giants and as a result probably know more about the War Between the States than any kid needs to.

In conclusion, I would like to offer sincere apologies to anyone I've failed to name. Please know that my heart is grateful, even if my memory sometimes fails. Thank you, Pelican, for your commitment to the truth, even when it isn't politically correct.

Finally, I offer deepest thanks to the Triune God whom I worship and seek to follow daily: God the Father's perfect plan of redemption, the Holy Spirit's convicting work, and Jesus Christ, who paid the price. It is only by the grace of God that cold-hearted, spiritually dead sinners like Nathan Bedford Forrest—and Shane Eric Kastler—can find eternal redemption and salvation. Any ability which I might have is a direct result of God's blessing upon my life. My greatest desire is for him to receive all praise and glory in the telling of this true story of a sinner's salvation. Thank you, Lord, for changing the lives of Forrest, myself, and countless others. May you be glorified in my life and in this book.

Introduction

"This is a faithful saying, and worthy of all acceptation, that Christ Jesus came into the world to save sinners; of whom I am chief." (1 Timothy 1:15 KJV)

On May 17, 1865, as the Civil War was drawing to a close, one of Nathan Bedford Forrest's hometown newspapers, the *Memphis Bulletin,* ran a front-page banner headline that read: "GENERAL FORREST KILLED." The story went on to report how Forrest had executed four of his troops without a trial for cheering at the news of Confederate general Joseph Johnston's surrender to Union general William Tecumseh Sherman. Then, as an act of vengeance, a group of Forrest's disgruntled men shot him down in response to the execution. There was only one problem with the newspaper story: the incident did not happen, and General Forrest most certainly was not dead. The next day the *Bulletin* ran a retraction stating that General Forrest had been seen alive and well and that their source had, in fact, been in error.[1]

Many citizens of Memphis must have been shocked by the headline that day since Forrest was a man with a knack for survival. Through four hard-fought years of war, Nathan Bedford Forrest had escaped death time and time again. In fierce hand-to-hand combat, he was known to have killed thirty men throughout the duration of the war. Exhibiting a fearless spirit and a taste for battle, he had led countless cavalry charges and raids, oftentimes against Federal forces that grossly outnumbered his own. He had witnessed many of his comrades, including his own brother, gunned down in

11

battle, yet through it all he survived. Sherman had stated that Forrest must be hunted down and killed if the Federals were to ever make any ground in Tennessee, famously stating, "That Devil Forrest must be killed if it costs 10,000 lives and breaks the Federal Treasury."[2] Sherman promised two Union officers generalships if they succeeded in assassinating Forrest. But, they never did succeed. Near the end of the war, during a savage hand-to-hand battle, Forrest fought off six would-be killers and then rode out with a seventh chasing him, wildly slashing at him with a saber. Eventually managing to draw his pistol, Forrest killed the man, his final casualty of the war. Indeed, Nathan Bedford Forrest seemed to be living a charmed life, or perhaps a divinely protected one. But was he worthy of such protection?

Most would say no. Growing up on a dirt poor frontier farm in Tennessee, Forrest was born the first of what would be fifteen children to Mariam Beck Forrest. At sixteen, young Bedford, who would always go by his middle name, became the man of the house upon his father's death. He helped to protect and provide for his mother and siblings until she eventually remarried and his brothers grew old enough to care for the farm.

As a young man, Bedford would go into business with his uncle in Hernando, Mississippi, where he would kill his first men, attackers of the sixty-five-year-old Jonathan Forrest. Eventually becoming a slave trader in Memphis, Forrest grew wealthy plying a trade that most, even in the South, considered to be a swarthy and notorious profession. He became a millionaire through his "Negro mart," plantations, and real estate acquisitions, eventually even garnering a certain amount of respect by being elected alderman on the Memphis City Council.

But Bedford Forrest had a knack for finding trouble and making enemies. The calm yet confident demeanor could transform into an explosive rage when tested and Forrest could be quick to throw a punch or pull a gun if his honor or his feelings were assaulted. Without doubt, Forrest was not someone you would consider a worthy candidate to receive grace from a holy and righteous God.

When the Civil War came along in 1861, Forrest's reputation, both for brave leadership and for unnecessary savagery, grew. Enlisting as a private with his brother Jeffrey and his fifteen-year-old son, William, in the Seventh Tennessee Cavalry, Bedford would quickly be promoted to lieutenant colonel and given the task of raising his own mounted regiment. Proving to be just as able a recruiter as he was a warrior, Forrest would inspire thousands of Southerners to fight to the death by his example, by his courage, and even by his intimidation. Eventually ascending to the rank of lieutenant general, the only man on either side to experience such a meteoric rise during the course of the war, Forrest would make his name famous and feared by the Northern army.

It was during the disputed events of the assault on Fort Pillow in April 1864 that Forrest's infamous legacy reached its crescendo. After calling on the Federals to surrender or face the sword, Forrest's men overtook Fort Pillow and killed many of the inhabitants, even after they had surrendered. Made up of "Tennessee Yankees" who had joined the Union army, Confederate deserters, and black Union soldiers, the Fort Pillow regiment certainly gained no measure of sympathy from Forrest's proud Southern troops. Yet the details, even today, are sketchy as to what took place and how much Forrest was involved. Regardless of this fact, he was skewered by Northern newspapers, and in many people's eyes, he would forever live in infamy as the "butcher of Fort Pillow."

If Forrest came out of the Civil War a villain in Northern eyes, he somehow managed to tarnish his reputation even further with his postwar involvement in the Ku Klux Klan. Though he is frequently and erroneously credited with founding the Klan, he was in fact not a member during its first year and a half of existence. And even after that his involvement is disputed. It seems clear that he had some organizational role as he traveled around the postwar South, and some have claimed him to be the first grand wizard of the Klan. Seen by its adherents as a paramilitary group to protect Southerners from radical Union Reconstructionists and former slaves, the Klan began to grow through the late 1860s, and with its numerical growth also came an increase in acts of violence conducted by some of its men. Bedford Forrest claimed that he renounced all measures of violence towards blacks, stating that his primary complaint was with the white, radical Republicans who were the cause of the strife. He called on the organization to disband following the 1868 elections, citing that their work was now complete. But it was not to be. The Klan would continue without Forrest.

However, Nathan Bedford Forrest's life story does not end with the Civil War, Southern racism, or the Ku Klux Klan. The waning years of Forrest's life brought a rather dramatic and surprising conversion to Christianity. Being raised by a devout Christian mother, and having married a pious Presbyterian girl, Forrest had a fair amount of Christian influence throughout his life. Nevertheless, he considered Christianity to be a woman's religion and claimed that he could not become a Christian when there was so much "unholy business" to do during the war. By all accounts, Forrest appeared to be one of those men who was content to let his women do his praying for him while he lived a reckless life of entangling sin. But that all changed in the 1870s.

As he neared the end of his life, Forrest began attending church with his wife and eventually made a public profession of faith in Christ, joining the Presbyterian church she attended. Under deep spiritual conviction and sorrow, after hearing a sermon on Jesus' parable of the two builders from Matthew 7, Forrest claimed to be the man who built his life on sand and sought God's forgiveness through Christ.

Having once been a racist, Nathan Bedford Forrest became an outspoken advocate of black civil rights in Memphis, culminating in his beautiful yet largely forgotten

speech before the black civil rights Pole-Bearers Association
in 1875. Encouraging the black people in attendance to take
an active part in their country's government, he told them
he was with them "heart and hand" to help their cause in any
way he could.

This is the untold story of Nathan Bedford Forrest. This
is the story of how the "chief of sinners" became a humble
saint. This is the story of how "that Devil Forrest," as General
Sherman called him, found eternal redemption in Jesus
Christ. This is the story of how a man, maligned even today
by many civil rights organizations as the epitome of Southern
white supremacy, was in fact, by the end of his days, one of the
black man's most faithful supporters. This is the story of how
God's grace, found in the gospel of Jesus Christ, can change
even the most callous and hardened of sinners and how that
very thing happened in the life of Nathan Bedford Forrest.

Another violent aggressor from world history once
terrorized people in his passion for a cause. Saul of Tarsus was
a Jewish zealot who lived in first-century Palestine and swore to
destroy a new religious sect calling themselves Christians. The
Christians claimed that the Messiah had come in the person of
Jesus of Nazareth and that many of the Jews had erroneously
rejected him. Saul's hatred for Jesus and his followers was so
intense that he sought to wipe them off the face of the Earth,
acquiring permission from the Jewish rulers to chase down
and imprison any Christians he found. As he approached
Damascus in pursuit of some of these Christians, Saul was
knocked from his horse by a light so bright it blinded him.
Then he heard a booming voice ask him: "Saul, Saul, why are
you persecuting Me? . . . I am Jesus whom you are persecuting,
but get up and enter the city, and it will be told to you what
you must do" (Acts 9:4-6 NASB). Something powerful and
quite unexpected happened to Saul. In this moment of divine
intervention, Saul became a new creature in Christ. A man
known for his violence, zeal, and intimidation began a life of
humility, service, and gospel ministry.

But some doubted his conversion was real. When he tried to fellowship with the Christian church in Jerusalem, they would have nothing to do with him. His reputation was well known and their natural fears got the better of them. It was not until a man named Barnabas came along and offered a recommendation and validation of Saul's true change that he was reluctantly accepted by the church (see Acts 9:26-29). As it turned out, the church's reluctance was unfounded, for this Saul who was so feared and dreaded by Christian society soon proved himself to be the Lord Jesus' most faithful and outspoken follower. He traveled the Middle Eastern world of his day taking the gospel to both Jew and Gentile. He was frequently beaten, imprisoned, chased, and persecuted for his Christian faith and salvation message, eventually being martyred for his Lord. Ironically, Saul of Tarsus, who once persecuted Christians, had himself become a persecuted Christian. With Saul's new life also came a new name. He began going by Paulos Apostolos, or as we would say in English, Paul the Apostle. Given the task of taking the gospel to the world, under the Holy Spirit's inspiration, he also penned half of the New Testament. This fearsome miscreant had become a fearless missionary. And the world has never been the same.

Paul's life, like that of Nathan Bedford Forrest's, gives us hope that God can indeed change the vilest of sinners. God can cleanse the dirtiest of hearts. God can humble the proudest of men. And God can forgive the most heinous offenders. But the question is, can we?

Nathan Bedford Forrest was a sinner, as we all are according to the Bible: "For all have sinned and fallen short of the glory of God" (Romans 3:23 NASB). And as sinners, our depravity manifests itself in various ways. Too often we like to justify ourselves with our "pet sins," which we consider to be less odious (at least in our eyes) than someone else's. We castigate the murderer while harboring hatred in our hearts. Or we gossip about the drunkard, forgetting that our gossip is also a sin in God's eyes. We proudly condemn the racist, ignoring that our pride and arrogance are sins as well. Forrest's sins were bad. He was a racist. He was arrogant. He liked to gamble. He used profanity. And perhaps the sin that he struggled with most and that subsequently led to many of his other sins was a hair-trigger temper that led him into many predicaments and countless physical confrontations. But no one, not even Nathan Bedford Forrest, is beyond the reach of God's grace through the gospel of Jesus Christ.

Many scoundrels throughout history have been thought to be beyond change, and yet God shocks the world by orchestrating their dramatic conversion. The aforementioned Saul of Tarsus became Paul the Apostle. Saint Augustine of Hippo was once a womanizing pagan before his tearful conversion and subsequent decades of service as a Christian bishop in northern Africa. John Newton was a profane British slave trader who found redemption in Christ and became a longtime Anglican pastor, author, and hymn writer. John Bunyan was a foul-mouthed, hot-tempered drunk before the Lord changed him into an outspoken gospel preacher and writer of one of the world's most beloved Christian allegories, *Pilgrim's Progress*. Charles Colson was Pres. Richard Nixon's "hatchet man," responsible for corrupt practices during the Watergate scandal, before God turned him into one of America's most consistent voices in defense of the Christian faith.

A careful examination of Nathan Bedford Forrest's life shows that we can add his name to this illustrious list of sinners turned saints by the power of God's gospel. At the end of the day, all Christians are merely sinners whom God has chosen to change into trophies of grace. And when we hear their stories, their testimonies, we are indeed inspired. For in the stories of divine redemption, we learn that change is in fact possible for anyone. We learn that God's power can overcome any personal failures. We learn that God's love can overcome any personal hatred. And we learn that God's grace is quite amazing.

This book tells the redemption story of one of those

hardened sinners, eternally changed by God's grace. And in this story we are reminded that anyone, even "that Devil Forrest," can be transformed into a worshipper, follower, and humble servant of the Lord Jesus Christ.

Chapter 1

Childhood Years on the Frontier

"Train up a child in the way he should go: and when he is old, he will not depart from it." (Proverbs 22:6 KJV)

Two ladies chatted peacefully as they rode their horses across the Tennessee countryside. Having enjoyed a nice visit to the neighbor's homestead, Mariam and her sister Fanny were now venturing the few miles home with a sack full of baby chicks in tow. Little did they know that their every step was being stalked by a large, hungry panther. Their pleasant ride ended when over the still sounds of nature they heard the hungry cat's low guttural growl, and immediately they spurred their mounts and began to gallop away from the danger.

"Mariam, he's after the chicks. Just drop 'em and let him have them. It's not worth our lives!" Fanny pleaded. "No way!" Mariam replied. "I won't be bullied by a panther . . . hungry or not!"

Their flight was successful until they rode within earshot of their cabin, where the horses had to slow down to cross the creek, giving the panther time to catch up. As they lumbered through the water, the panther pounced, sinking his front claws into Mariam's back as his back claws pierced the horse's flesh. Terrified, the horse bounded out of the creek while Mariam doggedly shook off the attacker—all the while clinging to her bag of baby chicks.

Shaken and bleeding, the ladies rode up to the house where Mariam's brood of children, led by the oldest son Bedford, came scurrying out to see the cause of the commotion. Though the panther could not have known, he made a grave error by singling out this pair of women to accost. For the fiercely stubborn woman's name was Mariam Beck Forrest, and her equally stubborn and resolute son was Nathan Bedford Forrest. The panther had come after his Ma, and Bedford would make the animal pay with his life.

In the 1800s, Tennessee frontier life was not a place for the faint of heart. Consequently, it was neither the weak nor the cowardly who abandoned the relative safety of the East Coast and set out to trailblaze west. Seeking land and a new life, many left New England, the Carolinas, Georgia, Virginia, and Maryland for the opportunities western pilgrimage offered. The Forrests of Orange County, North Carolina, were among these nomads. William Forrest, the father of Nathan Bedford, was eight years old when he arrived with his family in Middle Tennessee. William's father, Nathan Forrest, settled in Bedford County and made his living off the land. Eight children were born to Nathan and they all eventually made their living by selling livestock, except for two—William, who became a blacksmith, and another brother who became a tailor. Likewise, the Beck family migrated west from South Carolina in the late 1790s, eventually settling near Duck Creek, Tennessee, in 1796. Strong, hard-working Scotch-Irish Presbyterians, the Becks also made their livelihood by farming. In 1820 these two families merged with the marriage of William Forrest and Mariam Beck. Nearly six feet tall, Mariam was just a shade shorter than her six-foot, two-inch husband. Both were muscular, tough, hard-working, rough-hewn pioneers who had grown up accustomed to the adversity of frontier life.

In 1821, the Forrests had the first two of what would be eight children when twins were born on July 21. The daughter was named Frances, after her maternal Aunt Fanny, and the son was named after his grandfather and his birthplace. Nathan Bedford Forrest entered a world of abject poverty, born in a tiny, one-room log cabin. He would know early the twin traits of hard work and firm discipline.

Not much is known of William Forrest, though neighbors described him as an honest and clean-living man. Apparently not one to succumb to the common temptations of liquor or violence, Forrest seemed to be content working his blacksmith shop and raising his family. Mariam was the more dominant personality in the home and the provider of an early religious foundation. Like most frontier families of that generation, the Forrests expected absolute obedience from their children, and a sound whipping would greet the child who stepped out of line. Mariam never lost her belief in firm discipline, as shown by the well-known account of her whipping her eighteen-year-old son Joseph, a private in the Confederate army, for refusing to get out of bed when she called him. Mariam set down her coffee, walked outside, cut some switches off of a tree, doled out the punishment, and returned to the kitchen, commenting, "Soldier, or no soldier; my children will mind me as long as I live."[1]

When Bedford was thirteen, the family moved to Tippah County, Mississippi, and three years later, in 1837, William Forrest died, leaving sixteen-year-old Bedford as the male head of a household that included his mother and seven siblings. But the Forrests took the loss of William in stride and Bedford assumed the role of father figure and protector of the family. There was little time for sympathy, and no time for pity. Crops had to be planted. Animals had to be tended. And children had to be fed. He worked the land during the day, then came home and helped care for the children at night. His own recollection of this time was that "he would labor all day in the field and then at night sit up and work until it was late making buckskin leggings and shoes and coon-skin caps for his younger brothers."[2] He loved and protected his younger siblings. And he loved and protected his mother.

Mariam Forrest's panther attack occurred in the evening, near sunset, but that did not stop Bedford from whistling at his dogs, grabbing his rifle from over the mantle, and taking off after the cat. His mother pleaded with him to wait until morning, but he argued that the panther would be long gone by then and he intended to rid the Earth of such a creature. Clearly, Mariam's stubborn determination was passed on to her son, who tracked the animal all night, then killed it with one shot to the head. After scalping the cat, he brought the "trophy" home, presenting it to his mother as a gift.

In all likelihood, organized religion played a very minor role in the Forrest children's upbringing. Houses of worship were few and far between in the sparsely populated pioneer country of what was then known as America's West. The most common occasion for congregational worship would have been those rare occurrences when a circuit-riding preacher came to the area and conducted a service. As populations increased, so did congregations, but the "church on every corner" reality of today's American South was not the world in which Bedford Forrest grew up.

Though honest and hardworking, Bedford's father, William, was not known to be a religious man. We can not say with certainty that he was not a Christian; we simply do not have the information available. It appears that the majority of religious influence in the Forrest household would have come from Mariam. Mariam Forrest was devout, even though frontier life had left her a little rough around the edges. It was said that she "chewed tobacco, went to horse races, and spit as big as a man."[3] Of course in that day and age frontier women frequently chewed tobacco, and horse races were a common means of entertainment among the country people, not having the gambling stigma attached to it that it has today. Others describe Mariam as a God-fearing and honest woman who believed wholeheartedly in raising her children by the Biblical mandate towards "fear and admonition of the Lord."

While modern society often promotes overindulgence as a means of showing children love, the nineteenth-century rural world believed that firm discipline was necessary for a child's proper upbringing. Children were expected to pull their weight by working around the house and on the farm. They were to respect and obey their elders, especially their parents, and they could expect a swift whipping if they misbehaved. No doubt Mariam ruled her house with a rod of iron, but her children loved and respected her and knew that she loved them as well.

At the very least, the Forrest children were raised to have a healthy respect and fear of God. They were taught right from wrong, they were taught the righteousness of hard work and self-reliance, and they were taught that obedience brought reward while disobedience brought punishment. In many cases, frontier Christianity had a very simplistic, sometimes even superstitious nature and many believed that they were to simply do their best and God would reward them for it.

At this stage in his life, Forrest was forging a view that Christianity was for women. And while he later credited his safety in battle to the prayers of a faithful mother and wife, he took no active part in Christianity himself. If the ladies were praying for him, then God would protect him. If they were not, then he might not. At any rate, he was content for many years to live his spiritual life vicariously through his mother and wife.

While the young Bedford Forrest may not have modeled perfect piety, he does deserve respect for taking over the male leadership of his home at the age of sixteen and becoming a tremendous provider and protector. One well-known story involves a conversation Bedford had with a neighbor who could not seem to keep his ox from escaping and trampling though the Forrests' cornfield. Bedford confronted the neighbor over it, threatening to shoot the ox if it happened again. The headstrong and older neighbor promised to do the same to young Bedford if such action were taken. Not surprisingly, the ox escaped once more, and Bedford kept his word by gunning the animal down. The livid neighbor heard the shot and came running with gun in hand only to find Bedford reloading and taking aim at him. As the shot whizzed inches over his head, the neighbor scurried home, never again to question the mettle of Bedford Forrest.

By all accounts, the family farm flourished under Bedford's resolute oversight. He and his younger brothers worked the land, tended the animals, and harvested bountiful crops. Not only was Bedford a hard worker, but he also possessed rare acumen for leadership and organization, no doubt largely due to the fact that he was required to take the male lead over the family when his father died. In the "sink or swim" world that he was suddenly thrust into, he swam—and he swam admirably. The farm became such a success that he felt comfortable leaving it in the capable hands of his younger brothers to head out on his own adventure.

In 1841, a group of Mississippians went west to fight in Texas's war for independence from Mexico. Bedford's younger brother John had already seen some action, having been wounded and crippled for life by an enemy round. Unfortunately for Bedford, by the time he arrived in Texas, the hostilities had ended and his services were unneeded. He found work mauling rails only long enough to save the money to return home. His military prowess would have to await a future conflict.

By the early 1840s, Bedford felt secure enough in his family's welfare to leave the farm for good and set out to make his way in the world. A combination of factors played into this life change. First, his younger siblings had grown in age and ability enough to manage affairs on the farm. Then, in 1843 Mariam chose to remarry, giving her hand to a man named Joseph Luxley. Undoubtedly the protective Bedford knew and approved of Luxley to the extent that he felt safe placing the farm and his family in Luxley's care.

It was also about this time that a business opportunity arose for young Bedford. Jonathan Forrest, an uncle living in Hernando, Mississippi, offered him a share in his horse-trading business and Bedford jumped at the chance to make a better life for himself. Applying his well-honed traits of organization and hard work, he steadily increased the business's income and year after year improved his financial standing.

The young Bedford Forrest seemed to have a knack for three things: business, family honor, and violence. And these three converged on a fateful day in 1845. The Matlock boys rode into Hernando that day with revenge on their mind. Apparently, Jonathan Forrest owed the family money and either had not been able to pay or had not agreed on the amount. At any rate, they strolled into his establishment that day with plans to settle the score in blood. While the twenty-four-year-old Bedford had no desire to get sucked into a money squabble of his uncle's, he also refused to stand by and watch four men rough up sixty-five-year-old Jonathan. He made it clear that if a fight ensued, it would at least be four against two, rather than four against one. As tensions and words became more and more heated, one of the Matlocks pulled a gun and killed Jonathan with one shot to the chest. Unflinchingly, Bedford pulled a pistol and shot two of them where they stood. Still outnumbered two to one, and with no more bullets in his gun, Bedford appeared to be in over his head as he tussled with the remaining assailants. Then a bystander tossed him a bowie knife. He promptly attacked, injuring one before they fled the scene.

A subsequent trial found Bedford innocent of any wrongdoing. The court rightly determined that he was defending himself, but in so doing he had made quite an impression on the citizens of Hernando. In addition to being a local merchant, he was now also given the responsibility of being the town's lawman. That rare combination of physical skill and obvious leadership qualities had not only won him respect, it had won him another role as protector. But this time it was not just his family, it was the entire community.

Chapter 2

Mary Ann Montgomery:
The Saint Who Married the Devil

"Who can find a virtuous woman? For her price is far above rubies. The heart of her husband doth safely trust in her, so that he shall have no need of spoil. She will do him good and not evil all the days of her life." (Proverbs 31:10-12 KJV)

Mary Ann Montgomery was every boy's dream, and she was about to meet every father's nightmare. Mary Ann was petite; Bedford was rough hewn. Mary Ann was well educated; Bedford was uneducated. Mary Ann was quiet and well-mannered; Bedford was brash and confrontational. Mary Ann was devout; Bedford was profane. Nevertheless, providence had a plan that would bring these two most unlikely partners together.

On a beautiful Sunday morning, Mary Ann and her mother rode in their carriage to church. At least it was a beautiful day until they encountered the muddy creek. Halfway through, their driver became stuck, and regardless of how hard he and the horses tried, they were unable to budge the buggy. To make matters worse, two young men stood on the bank enjoying a hearty laugh at the spectacle. Onto this scene rode the proverbial knight in shining armor who would soon take care of both situations.

The young, handsome Nathan Bedford Forrest called out to the ladies stuck in the wagon and asked for permission to carry them to shore. After gaining their approval he waded out to the middle of the creek and carried nineteen-year-old Mary Ann and her mother to the safety of the bank. It would be foolish to underestimate the effect this event had on Mary Ann. Here was

27

a tall, handsome, muscular man who was willing to give up his comfort to save the damsels in distress. And to do so while the ladies were in the very midst of ridicule from two other males of less stellar quality added to the chivalry. Bedford Forrest had impressed Mary Ann, but his work was not quite finished. Once again he returned to the creek and pressed hard against the back of the buggy until he and the driver were able to break it free. The driver rode onto the shore, and while the ladies once again climbed aboard the wagon, Bedford made a beeline for the two troublesome hecklers. After blasting them for their lack of chivalry, he told them in no uncertain terms that they had best leave or he would give them the whipping of their lives. As they scurried away, Bedford ran back to the wagon and asked the older woman if he could have her permission to call on her daughter sometime. Grateful for his help, Mrs. Montgomery probably felt she had no choice but to oblige, and so began a relationship that would last for the rest of their earthly days.

Mary Ann and Bedford were polar opposites in just about every way conceivable. She would be considered quite a catch for any young man, and apparently Bedford was well aware of this, as were the two young men who had refused to help when the ladies were stuck in the creek. The very next day, Bedford Forrest made his way to the Montgomery home to call upon Mary Ann. When he was shown into the parlor he found that there were already two other young men waiting to see her. In fact, they were the same two boys who witnessed Mary Ann's creek adventure and chose to laugh rather than help. Maybe they were there to apologize or explain themselves. Maybe one of them had a romantic interest in her. Or maybe they just wanted to pass the time of day. Whatever they wanted, they never got the chance to say. Forrest promptly sent them packing once more with yet another threat of violence if they dared to show their faces around there again. When Mary Ann finally appeared, there was only one man waiting to meet her. This tall, strapping backwoodsman whom she had just met the day before was there announcing his desire to have her hand in marriage. We do not know whether she was shocked, flattered, or excited—probably a combination of the three.

Mary Ann has sometimes been called the daughter of a Presbyterian minister but that is not quite right. She was in fact the niece of a Presbyterian minister, but due to the fact that her father had died, Uncle Samuel Cowan assumed the primary role as male guardian in her life. While we may not know Mary Ann's reaction to Forrest's proposal, what we do know is that Samuel Cowan was not impressed. Apparently, Reverend Cowan knew Forrest, if not personally, then surely by reputation. The idea of his beautiful Christian niece linking up with the likes of Bedford Forrest made his flesh crawl, and he was not bashful about making that clear. "Why Bedford I couldn't consent to your marrying her. You cuss and gamble, and Mary Ann is a good Christian girl," Cowan argued. "I know she is," Bedford replied. "That's why I want to marry her." Bedford promised that he would provide, love, and care for her. He assured the minister that he would never have to give a second's worry to her well-being, for he would be a faithful husband and a good provider.

Maybe Cowan knew some of Forrest's history. The way he had become the man of the house at sixteen and cared for his mother and siblings would impress anyone. He no doubt also knew the details of the altercation involving Jonathan Forrest and how Bedford had come to the aid of his aged uncle. Clearly he was a brave and valiant man. Or maybe Samuel Cowan could simply see that his niece had fallen in love with Bedford Forrest. Whatever it was that made him consent, he eventually gave his approval and performed the wedding ceremony himself a mere six weeks after Mary Ann and Bedford met.

From a Biblical standpoint, the union of Nathan Bedford Forrest and Mary Ann Montgomery was a complete disaster. While our emotions may want us to get caught up in the love story, Scripture clearly teaches that a Christian and a non-Christian should not yoke themselves together in matrimony. The Bible says: "Do not be bound together with unbelievers; for what partnership have righteousness and lawlessness, or what fellowship has light with darkness? Or what harmony has Christ with Belial, or what has a believer in common with an unbeliever?" (2 Corinthians 6:14-15 NASB). At this point in his life Bedford might have claimed to be a Christian. And while he certainly adhered to the validity of Christianity, his life showed that his intellectual consent to the faith had not touched his heart to any lasting degree. Samuel Cowan clearly thought that to be the case, which is why he initially objected to their marriage. But it is within situations like this that the awe-inspiring sovereignty of God often comes into play.

Scripture gives numerous accounts of times in which people make mistakes and even willingly commit grievous sins, yet God uses it for his greater glory and their ultimate good. In the Old Testament we are told of a man named Joseph who was sold into slavery by his ten jealous brothers. Returning home without him, they lied to their father, saying that Joseph had been eaten by a lion. And while Joseph lived his life in Egypt the brothers lived with their lie for years on end. Eventually, Joseph worked his way up to a place of power in Egypt and because of the blessings of God in his life foretold a great famine that would come to the land. He stored up grain to preserve many lives, and his brothers eventually had to appear before him to beg for food. Although they did not recognize him at first, he soon revealed himself to them and understandably they feared for their very lives. But Joseph allayed their fears and comforted them, saying, "As for you, you meant evil against me, but God meant it for good in order to bring about this present result, to preserve many people alive" (Genesis 50:20 NASB).

Likewise are we told in the New Testament that Jesus Christ came as "God in the flesh" to live a perfect life and die a sacrificial death. As the second member of the Trinity,

Jesus was God the Son—and yet he was murdered. No greater evil could exist for mortal man than that he should murder the very Son of God. And yet in this act of supreme treachery, God's greater plan of redemption for his people was being carried out, for it was on the cross that Jesus paid the price and absorbed the Father's righteous wrath in place of those who would turn to Christ in faith. As the apostle Peter testified in his famous sermon on the day of Pentecost: "Men of Israel, listen to these words: Jesus the Nazarene, a man attested to you by God with miracles and wonders and signs which God performed through Him in your midst, just as you yourselves know—this Man, delivered over by the predetermined plan and foreknowledge of God, you nailed to a cross by the hands of godless men and put Him to death" (Acts 2:22-23 NASB). Indeed, many things in this world are bad, but God still chooses to use them for good.

And so it was with the marriage of the pious Mary Ann Montgomery and the sinful, though respectable Nathan Bedford Forrest. No Christian minister could in good conscience, based on Scriptural teaching, advise the two to become one, but no believer in the sovereignty of God could deny that this marriage would have a profound impact on Bedford Forrest's life.

It is easy to imagine the frustrations Mary Ann Forrest might have endured because of her husband. He had some admirable qualities to be sure: he was a good worker and a tremendous provider financially. He was also faithful and by all accounts gentle with his wife. But he was no Christian, while she was devout. Her life was lived for the glory of God. His life was lived in the pursuit of money, land, power, and respect. But, with all his faults, one is amazed at the amount of vices he managed to avoid.

In a time and place in which liquor flowed freely, Bedford was a complete teetotaler. He confessed that once as a teenager he had succumbed to the temptation and went to the woods with a bottle of whiskey to experiment with what it was like to be drunk. He passed out and woke up deathly sick, promising God that if he managed to get better he would never touch the stuff again. And he never did, except twice during the war when he was told by a doctor to take a drink for medicinal purposes. One of his aides during the war said that Forrest did not know the difference between whiskey and brandy and simply called it all liquor. When offered a drink, as he frequently was, he would decline and sometimes joke, "My staff does all my drinking for me." Furthermore, he had no use whatsoever for tobacco. He neither chewed, nor smoked, and he was well known to show a pristine set of pearly white teeth when he smiled.

He also seems to have been completely faithful regarding his marriage vows to Mary Ann. Though he was a strikingly handsome man who spent much time away from his wife, no credible story has ever been uncovered accusing him of marital infidelity. He seems to have been completely committed to Mary Ann and lived his life as a one-woman man.

But Bedford had his vices, and they had to have caused Mary Ann fits. Bedford loved to gamble, and throughout his life this proved to be one of his greatest struggles. Mary Ann despised it as being a gross dishonor to God and a poor example of stewardship. Sometimes she would plead with him not to go to the card tables, but he went nonetheless. And she would silently go to her room and pray for her wayward husband.

He also struggled with profanity, especially when he lost his temper. But even though he could blurt out the occasional four-letter word, one of his fellow soldiers testified that he abhorred any smutty talk and would not tolerate any jokes that were degrading to women. No doubt his deep love for his wife and mother attributed to this fact.

And so, Nathan Bedford Forrest has aptly been called an enigma.[1] He was a strange combination of bravado and gentleness, of violence and peace, of hard work and laxity, of financial success and financial squander. He was a gambler who did not drink, a fighter who did not smoke, and a cusser who did not like dirty jokes. At times, he was a walking contradiction and impossible to figure out. He possessed many sterling qualities, yet he also struggled with numerous sins.

Of all the sins Bedford Forrest fought, perhaps the greatest one (and the one that led to so many others) was his legendary temper. This one aspect of his character would bring him tremendous grief, and it was something he would struggle with all his life. For the most part, he was a fairly calm man, but when his fuse was lit he seemed to become another person. Almost in a Jekyll and Hyde fashion, his entire countenance and coloring would change. His face would glow, his eyes would flash red, and Bedford Forrest would explode in rage. But Mary Ann could change that. In fact, it was said that no matter how furious he got, she had the ability to calm him down with a mere word, a quality that Mariam Forrest also had over her son while he was growing up. Though he at times hated men who caused him trouble, he so revered and loved the women in his life that his violent tirades seem to have never been directed towards them.

After their wedding, Bedford and Mary Ann settled down in a small log cabin in Hernando, where he worked several different jobs. In addition to being elected town coroner, which in those days was a job that mainly required him to collect fines and serve warrants, he also worked in the mercantile business. Young, restless, and longing for fortune, Forrest tried several different businesses in an effort to strike it rich. He operated a stagecoach service to Memphis and sold cattle and horses. Eventually he found the trade that would make him wealthy and infamous. Forrest became a slave trader.

Slave trading was an interesting business in the prewar South. Though the region relied on slave labor to work the farms and plantations, most people considered the occupation of slave trader to be slimy and underhanded. Many Southern slaves had served the same family for generations and if they were not exactly considered part of the family, there was often a level of attachment between the white slaveholder and those who served him. The buying and selling of slaves was a shameful reminder of the realities of the human chattel system, a reminder that most Southern gentlemen preferred to avoid. But Forrest was utterly unconcerned with reputation and began working in earnest to make his fortune.

From a spiritual standpoint, what was going in Bedford Forrest's life at this time was the very same thing that goes on in many young people's lives, even those who were raised in Christian families. The lure of worldly prosperity draws people away from the faith they were taught. A young man like Forrest begins to see dollar signs everywhere he looks, and his youthful exuberance and energies are focused almost entirely on climbing the financial ladder. While money in and of itself is not bad, and hard work is commended by Scripture, the "love of money" is roundly condemned by the word of God. The apostle Paul wrote, "For the love of money is a root of all sorts of evil, and some by longing for it have wandered away from the faith and pierced themselves with many griefs" (1 Timothy 6:10 NASB). Would Bedford Forrest have been better off if he had never become a slave trader? Would he have been better off if he had simply raised crops and a family like his father had? Would he have been better off poor and pious as opposed to wealthy and wicked? Certainly he would have. But pride and ambition churned greatly within his soul. Growing up poor made him that much more determined to avoid poverty as an adult, and scruples meant little to him at this time. If selling humans brought him the financial security he longed for, then so be it. To him, slavery was not a moral issue. It was a legal and financial issue and it was a fact of life. Somebody was going to get rich selling slaves. He figured it might as well be him.

In Matthew 7, Jesus told the parable of the two builders, in which he states:

Therefore everyone who hears these words of Mine and acts on them, may be compared to a wise man who built his house on the rock. And the rain fell, and the floods came, and the winds blew and slammed against that house; and yet it did not fall, for it had been founded on the rock. Everyone who hears these words of Mine and does not act on them, will be like a foolish man who built his house on the sand. The rain fell, and the floods came, and the winds blew and slammed against that house; and it fell—and great was its fall. (Matthew 7:24-27 NASB)

A rare photograph of a prewar Forrest in civilian attire.

At this point in his life, though he did not realize it, Bedford was building his house upon the sand. His focus was on building an earthly, temporal fortune—a house that would not stand in eternity. His greatest need was to relinquish control of his life to Jesus Christ, to "hear these words of mine and act upon them," as Jesus said. But Forrest's fleshly pride blinded him to spiritual realities.

Eventually, the slave business would lead Forrest away from Hernando to the larger city of Memphis, where his work promised to be more lucrative. In 1851, he moved there with Mary Ann and their two children, William, born in 1846, and Frances, named after Forrest's twin sister, born in 1848. In Memphis, Forrest expanded the slave operation, partnering with several different businessmen over the years. He also began to acquire real estate, purchasing a large plantation in northern Mississippi.

Forrest's slave trading would often take him away from Memphis, and it was most likely business that took him to Texas in 1852. While heading home aboard a steamboat, passing near Galveston, Forrest tossed and turned in his bed as a cohort of drunken gamblers reveled in the ship's saloon. True to his form, Forrest marched in half-dressed and ordered the men to keep the noise down. Surprisingly they apologetically complied, no doubt influenced by the sleepy-eyed, forceful spectacle they saw before them. Still agitated, Forrest decided to take a walk on the deck of the ship, and in so doing he noticed the ship's boilers were overheating and the ship was moving at a tremendous speed. What's more, another ship was alongside them, also running at full throttle. Forrest rushed to the wheel room, where he found a drunken captain engaged in a race with the other vessel. Though Forrest pleaded with the man to slow down lest the ship go up in flames, the captain would not be deterred. He vowed to win the race, regardless of what happened to him or the ship. Forrest made his way to the back of the ship, hoping the boilers would hold but expecting them to explode. Within minutes, the sky was illuminated with the explosion of the ship's boilers, and mass carnage ensued. No one escaped without injury, and sixty people perished in the blast, but Forrest survived the ordeal. Inflicted with an injured shoulder, he helped with the wounded and the recovery of the dead as the other steamer came alongside to offer support.

For whatever reason, God had providentially preserved Forrest's life. It was not the first time, and it certainly would not be the last. While his inability to sleep that night irked him, it probably saved his life even as many others perished. His time had not yet come, and though he was as worthy of death as any, God chose to spare him, at least for now. God allowed Forrest to live, but rather than relinquish control of his life to God, Forrest would continue to amass his fortune selling slaves.

Although the modern mind rightly recoils at the thought of slavery, Forrest lived in different times. And while the days in which he lived cannot excuse all his sins, it can certainly explain some of them. White supremacist views were common in the day, in both the North and the South. Abolitionists were few and far between, and while some were uncomfortable with the "peculiar institution" of slavery, most did not question it. And no one questioned white superiority. Even the Great Emancipator, Abraham Lincoln, stated in one of his famous 1858 debates with Stephen A. Douglas that he did not think the black man "my equal in many respects, certainly not in color—perhaps not in moral or intellectual endowments."[2] White superiority was the rule of the day throughout the Union. Thus, in this sense, Forrest was simply a man of his times, trying to make a fortune in a business that many disapproved of, but few dared question its legitimacy.

For what it is worth, Forrest seems to have been kind to his slaves. While it was common practice to separate families, Forrest refused to do so, insisting on selling them in groups. Furthermore, he seems to have allocated them a certain amount of freedom, encouraging them to go out into the city to find their own masters and persuade the would-be slave owners to buy them. He also seems to have, for the most part, avoided the common practice of whipping slaves. Not surprisingly, slaves with numerous scars brought less money since they gave the appearance of being defiant and unruly. Therefore, Forrest had a financial stake in keeping the slaves content and well cared for. But his care extended beyond their basic needs to their health and appearance. He kept them clean, well fed, and housed. He provided medical care and showed them benevolence. It was said that the slaves respected Forrest but also feared him. Much as he behaved toward the men who served with him in combat, he was no doubt easy to get along with when everything went his way but could grow quickly angry when things did not. As a general rule, as slave traders went, Forrest seems to have been one of the better ones.

Though slave trading was considered fairly low class, Forrest gained a certain amount of respect when he was elected a city alderman in 1857. In this role, he flourished, even if at times he wrestled to control his legendary temper. Serving on the finance committee, he was meticulous on matters both great and small. On one occasion, the aldermen were called upon to inspect a bridge they had contracted. As they were walking across it, the lead alderman informed those closest to him that they should condemn the bridge so they could award a new contract to a friend of his. Presumably they were in agreement, until they approached Forrest with the idea. When told of their plans to condemn the bridge, Forrest argued that it appeared to be in good shape and that he saw no reason to condemn it. They then informed him of the reason, and Forrest's legendary temper ignited: "You infernal scoundrel! Do you dare to ask me to be as damned a rascal as yourself? I have a big notion to pitch you into the Mississippi River. Now, I warn you if you ever presume to address such a damnable proposition to me in the future

I will break your rascally neck."[3] Forrest may have had his faults, but dishonesty was not one of them.

Beginning around 1858, Forrest began to close down his slave selling business. As the rumbles of a potential Civil War began to sound, Forrest might have concluded that slavery was a dying business. He stepped down as alderman and decided to move Mary Ann and William (his daughter Frances died at age five in 1853) to his Mississippi plantation. Mary Ann probably played a part in this move. In Memphis, Forrest was a frequent visitor to the poker tables, where he would gain and lose money by the thousands. In addition to the financial perils of gambling, a moral stigma was attached, especially on the occasions when Forrest would be cited by the authorities for "playing cards," as he was in 1859. So, it was decided that a return to the country and the farm would do him good. He would keep busy overseeing the plantation, he would be free from the stresses of municipal government, and he would have a reputable occupation. His days of peaceful planting were destined to be short lived, however.

In November 1860, Abraham Lincoln was elected president of the United States, and immediate plans for Southern secession were put in place. State after state began to secede while Forrest held his peace. Initially, Tennessee and several other states remained in the Union. Though Lincoln's election concerned them, they were willing to try and make things work, but once Lincoln put out a call for 75,000 volunteers to "suppress the Southern rebellion," Tennessee joined her fellow Southerners in secession. Rather than intimidating the South into submission, Lincoln's call managed to fan the already smoldering flames of Southern patriotism. Like many Southern men, Forrest saw his duty to serve his native state, and with both Tennessee and Mississippi seceding, Forrest promptly enlisted along with his brother Jeffrey and son, William, all three mustering in as privates in the Tennessee cavalry.

No doubt Mary Ann's prayers increased as she watched her husband and only surviving child march off to war. Little did she or anyone else know that it would be four long years of hard-fought, bitter warfare before they marched back home again.

Chapter 3

Forrest Goes to War: 1861-1862

"He teacheth my hands to war, so that a bow of steel is broken by mine arms. Thou hast also given me the shield of thy salvation: and thy right hand hath holden me up, and thy gentleness hath made me great." (Psalms 18:34-35 KJV)

Tennessee had the distinction of being the last Southern state to leave the Union and the first to rejoin it. Though many of its citizens were fiercely proud and loyal to the South, other parts of the state had pockets of Union sympathizers. Bedford Forrest himself had been a strong Union man right up until the election of Abraham Lincoln as president. Forrest deeply desired a peaceful resolution to restore order to the nation, but when secession became inevitable, he left no doubt where his ultimate allegiance stood. If Tennessee would be part of the Confederacy, so would Nathan Bedford Forrest.

In June 1861, the nearly forty-year-old Bedford, along with his twenty-four-year-old brother Jeffrey and fifteen-year-old son William, joined the Tennessee Mounted Rifles, a cavalry regiment being formed under Josiah White. All three mustered in as privates, but Bedford would not remain a private very long.

Several factors played into Forrest's meteoric rise to lieutenant colonel in July 1861, not the least of which was his relationship with Gov. Isham Harris. Having both lived in the Memphis area for many years, Harris as a lawyer and Forrest as a slave trader and alderman, they were no doubt well acquainted in both political and social circles. While not everyone held a favorable view of Forrest, most agreed that he

The most well-known photograph of Forrest, taken early in the Civil War.

was a natural born leader, utterly fearless, excellent at getting things done, and perhaps most importantly, he had money. One of his hometown newspapers, the *Avalanche,* wrote an editorial in July pleading for a force of mounted rangers to be assembled who could protect Tennessee's borders as well as make raids into Union territory as needed. The article went on to suggest none other than Nathan Bedford Forrest to serve as its leader, having heard that many young men desired to serve under the well-known Memphis citizen. Governor Harris apparently concurred and gave Forrest the charge of forming his own cavalry regiment to serve the state and ultimately the Confederacy. A July 25, 1861, advertisement in the *Memphis Avalanche* made the following announcement:

A CHANCE FOR ACTIVE SERVICE—MOUNTED RANGERS
Having been authorized by Governor Harris to raise a battalion of mounted rangers for the war, I desire to enlist five hundred able-bodied men, mounted and equipped with such arms as they can procure (shot-guns and pistols preferable), suitable to the service . . .

—N.B. Forrest[1]

It was not long before many men wanted to serve in Forrest's cavalry, but horses, saddles, and guns were a different matter. While the government's offer to supply equipment was genuine, Forrest was not willing to wait and rely upon the state to furnish his men with supplies. He would make it happen from his own pocket and by risking his own neck. Within a matter of days, Bedford set off for Kentucky to outfit his newly formed battalion. Using both business and personal contacts, he was able to buy saddles, guns, and horses for his men. But getting them out of Kentucky and safely home to Tennessee would require some audacious maneuvering, as well as a little bit of bluffing. He sent his supply of saddles to a leather goods shop and had them placed in crates marked "leather." Surely the Yankees would not be suspicious of "leather" leaving a tannery. But what about guns being shipped in boxes marked "potatoes"? It was a gamble he was willing to take, and it ultimately paid off.

Knowing that he was being watched closely, Bedford rode into Louisville near dusk and made himself seen around town. At the same time, some of his men began the journey south with contraband in tow. With all suspicious eyes in town on him, no one knew that just a few miles away, the great caper was going down. Once nightfall came and the city fell into its slumber, Forrest quietly slipped out of town and caught up with his wagon train.

Supplies were not the only thing Bedford managed to land in Kentucky. Many new recruits also signed up for his cavalry and began to travel south with him. This gave him more men to help defend against any trouble, but it also aroused Yankee suspicion. Near the town of Munfordville, Kentucky, he was warned by some of his contacts that a Union cavalry regiment awaited him in town with plans to block his way, so Forrest put his backwoods smarts to use. He knew that a train would be passing them soon on its way to town, so he took his handful of cavalry soldiers, as well as their families, and sat close enough to the tracks to be seen but not close enough to be seen well. They appeared to be a rather large detachment of soldiers when in fact they were a small group of soldiers accompanied by loved ones. Nevertheless, Forrest knew that the train's passengers would immediately warn the Yankees in town upon their arrival. Realizing that the Yankee cavalry was most likely made up of green recruits like his own, he suspected they would not be willing to risk a fight with a Southern troop that greatly outnumbered them. His gamble, once again, paid off and they passed through the area unmolested.[2]

In the early days of the war, in 1861, Forrest's Rangers, as they came to be called, spent much of their time getting organized and patrolling western Tennessee and Kentucky. On one occasion, near the town of Marion, Kentucky, a woman found Forrest and told him about her husband, a

Confederate sympathizer, being arrested by the Union. Immediately he tracked down and arrested two of the Federals and sought to apprehend a third man by the name of Jonathan Bell. As Forrest and his surgeon, Dr. S. M. Van Wick, approached Bell's house, the Federal took a rifle shot at the doctor, who was dressed in his best military garb. Apparently he assumed Van Wick to be Colonel Forrest and unknowingly killed the wrong man. Forrest, quite literally, dodged a bullet that should have killed him, and Bell escaped. Bedford now resorted to plan B.

Finding a group of Baptist ministers on their way home from a conference, Forrest arrested eight of them and sent the remaining two into town with the threat that he would hang the others if the Confederate man was not released within twenty-four hours. Even though Forrest was likely bluffing, the plan worked and all parties were subsequently freed. Biographer Jack Hurst states, "It was inconsistent with his usual attitude towards clergy. Except for the times he chased the ministerial student away from Mary Ann Montgomery back in 1845, and this wartime incident sixteen years later, his normal treatment of men of God is reported to have been markedly respectful, despite his non-acceptance of the faith."[3]

Sacramento

The occasional minor skirmish with Union men was about all the action Forrest's Rangers saw until December of that year. Forrest was informed by some of his scouts that a Yankee cavalry regiment was about seven miles away from them, near the town of Sacramento, Kentucky. Immediately, Forrest and his men set off with the adrenalin-induced vigor of a likely fight. As they approached Sacramento, a teenage girl ventured out to find Forrest and warn him of the Federals, pleading for his help. Always respectful of females, he recorded in his official report that the young lady's brave act had the effect of "infusing nerve into my arm and kindling knightly chivalry within my heart."[4] In other words, Colonel Forrest felt sorry for the girl and was inspired to defend her and the others of her community against the dreaded Yankees.

It was at Sacramento that Forrest had his first taste of real battle and proved he was a master of military tactics although he had no training in them whatsoever. His brilliance on the field was not learned at West Point, nor any other classroom, and he did not know proper military terms, even if he masterfully employed the tactics. Instead of calling for flank attacks, he would say, "Boys, hit 'em on the end." Instead of calling his troops to engage the enemy, he would say, "Let's go mix with 'em, boys." He was a rugged Southern frontiersman who knew how to live off the land, protect himself, and fight.

Approaching the Northerners, Forrest gathered his men and informed them of his plan. He would divide his small army into three groups with one flanking the Union left, one flanking the Union right, and the third, led by Forrest himself, charging directly at the enemy. The scheme had the desired effect, and the Yankees began retreating towards town, with Forrest's Rangers in hot pursuit.

Forrest's charges were always intimidating because he told the men to "show fight." He believed that the more aggressively they came at the enemy, the more likely the enemy would retreat or surrender. Even when Forrest had fewer numbers, he knew that a show of aggression would make it seem as if he had more men than he did. And the sight of Forrest himself put the fear of God in Yankees. At six feet, two inches, he was far taller than the average man of his day, but he would seem even more gigantic by standing in the stirrups of his horse during battle. With a face flushed red with excitement; piercing eyes; a jet black, pointed goatee; and steel gray hair, it is no surprise he was called a devil. One glimpse of him in battle could cripple a soldier with fear.

Nevertheless, at one point in the Battle of Sacramento, he found himself in a precarious situation as he fought with sabers against three Yankee officers. Forrest was surrounded

and in serious trouble when Pvt. W. H. Terry rode up to help his colonel. Terry's presence momentarily distracted one of the Yankees, who shot Terry, killing him instantly. This gave Forrest just enough time to turn and kill one of the Yankees and wound another before escaping. Forrest had evaded another brush with death in what would be one of many during the war.

While Forrest fought on the western front, in the east another Confederate began his ascent to worldwide fame. During the Battle of First Manassas, Virginia's little-known Tom Jackson stood like a stone wall defending a portion of the battlefield known as Henry House Hill. From then on, Jackson would be forever immortalized as "Stonewall" because of his uncanny ability to stand calmly in battle, even as bullets whizzed past him. In fact, at Manassas a bullet injured his hand, yet Jackson managed to stay serene when everything else around him was chaotic. A captain in his brigade questioned him about this peculiar trait after the battle, and Jackson gave the reason for his calm: "Captain, my religious belief teaches me to feel as safe in battle as in bed. God has fixed the time for my death. I do not concern myself about that, but to be always ready, no matter when it may overtake me."[5]

Jackson was clinging to the Bible's promise of Psalm 139, which states, "Your eyes have seen my unformed substance; and in Your book were all written the days that were ordained for me, when as yet there was not one of them" (Psalms 139:16 NASB). God alone determines the day of one's death, and he in his perfect providence will see that it comes to pass. Jackson firmly believed this at the very core of his being and could therefore remain cool in battle, knowing that if God had appointed him to die that day, nothing could prevent it. And likewise if God had ordained him to survive that day, then all the Yankees in the world could not take his life. Jackson rested in the sovereignty of God over death and lived until his "appointed day" came in May 1863.

Ironically, Forrest did not honor God with his life as Jackson did but still reaped the benefits of God's divine protection and in many ways shared Jackson's fearlessness in the face of death. The providence of God is difficult for mortal man to comprehend. Yet it is the clear teaching of Scripture that God exercises omnipotent control over our world, and our days are ordained by him. Private Terry's time had come. But in the providence and the grace of God, Nathan Bedford Forrest would live to fight another day.

Fort Donelson

That day would come a mere two months later at Fort Donelson, Tennessee. Seeing the strategic importance of Fort Henry and Fort Donelson, separated by just twelve miles, with Henry on the banks of the Tennessee River and Donelson on the banks of the Cumberland River, Union general Ulysses S. Grant attacked Fort Henry. Confederate general Lloyd Tilgham quickly saw the handwriting on the wall and sent the majority of his twenty-five hundred men to Fort Donelson, leaving only a handful of artillery gunners to defend Fort Henry, which surrendered on February 6, 1862. Tilgham planned to parlay as many troops as possible at Donelson with hopes of sustaining a defense there.

On February 12, the Federals began their march from Henry towards Donelson, but they were slowed somewhat by Forrest's cavalry, who harassed them with constant fire. Later that evening the Union gunboat U.S.S. *Carondelet* arrived at the fort by way of the Cumberland River and began to shell Fort Donelson. Bedford Forrest helplessly watched the fort get pummeled from a nearby hill. Sitting next to him was Capt. David C. Kelley from Hunstville, Alabama, who just a few minutes prior had been back with his men reading his Bible.

David C. Kelley would prove to be one of Forrest's most trusted subordinates during the war. When the war began in 1861, Kelley was serving as pastor of the First Methodist Church of Huntsville and had previously served two years as a missionary to China. In addition to being a cavalry officer, he

David C. Kelley, who served as a faithful subordinate to Forrest for much of the war. Eventually rising to the rank of colonel, he had been a Methodist pastor and missionary to China prior to the war. He served as chaplain and frequently preached in Forrest's camp. His chaplain's assistant was Forrest's son, William. (Courtesy of Huntsville-Madison County Library, Huntsville, Alabama)

also served Forrest's Rangers as a chaplain and frequently led worship services with the men. At Mary Ann's request, and with Bedford's blessing, young William Forrest had become Kelley's ministerial assistant. For the duration of the war, William would gather the men when it was time for worship, and he would assist Kelley in whatever way he could with the service. Having become a Christian at a young age, William had a temperament and personality more like his mother's than his father's. He was brave but quiet. A fearless soldier who would go wherever his father commanded him, he was also a faithful believer who would do whatever his heavenly Father commanded him.

When he enlisted as a fifteen year old at the beginning of the war, William was initially refused by the army because of his youth, but through his father's influence he was given a place of service as an assistant on Bedford's staff. Undoubtedly Mary Ann worried about her only son, about not only his safety, but also the influences that might affect him in military life. One day early in the war, Bedford's staff was surprised to see him ride up with two teenage boys he had requested from commanding general Leonidas Polk. They did not seem to have any real need for the well-mannered, clean-cut boys, but Bedford had plans for them. Polk was a bishop in the Episcopal Church, so Forrest had approached him, requesting a couple of young, devout Christians who might serve on his staff. What Forrest really wanted were a couple of friends for William, friends who would encourage him in his faith rather than serve as stumbling blocks to it. While Forrest may have been profane at times, he did not want his son to mimic him. William was like Mary Ann, who was like Christ in her attitude—and that is the way Bedford wanted it.

On one occasion, while bivouacking in western Tennessee, Colonel Forrest was joined by his mother, who sat with him while Reverend Kelley led a worship service. After Mariam Forrest left for home, Kelley went to Forrest's tent to visit, where he found that Mariam had left her well-worn Bible with her son in hopes that he would read it.

Captain Kelley's faith had a tremendous effect upon his men, and probably Forrest as well. Kelley encouraged the troops with his personal motto: "In the path of duty there is no danger." J. C. Blanton, who served under Kelley, stated, "Kelley walked . . . amid the roar of artillery, the rattle of musketry, even mid the groans of the dying as calmly as he had formerly walked to his pulpit on Sabbath morning. D. C. Kelley was one of the bravest men I ever saw. I never saw him manifest the least sign of fear or excitement on any field of battle, and I was with him on many."[6] Blanton told of an incident during the early part of the Fort Donelson bombardment when the cavalry were given orders to stand down and await further instructions. During the lull, Kelley pulled out his Bible and began to read. Blanton recounts:

> Our regiment being cavalry could not be used in defense of the fort. So we were placed back to wait for orders. During this bombardment and when it looked like the furies of hell were turned loose on us, I looked down the line, and saw Kelley sitting on a camp stool leaning against a tent pole reading his Bible. My curiosity was at once excited, and wondering if it were possible for a man to be interested even in reading God's word under such circumstances, I walked to where he was, stood close to him until I was satisfied that he was deeply interested in the Book. I went back and called some comrades' attention to it, and after going close to him they returned in perfect amazement, that any man could be so composed amid such roaring of cannon shots, and screaming shells. Why, the very earth was quivering under us.[7]

Kelley had a better opportunity to judge Forrest than most because of their close relationship during the war, and the picture Kelley paints is that Forrest was a deep respecter of the things and people of God but more of a lukewarm observer than an active partaker in the faith. Kelley states:

> Throughout the war he always gave me the fullest opportunit-
> ies for preaching in camp, courteously entertaining at his mess
> table all preachers whom I might choose to invite. He was
> always present at such services when it was practicable. While
> we were messmates there was always family prayer in his tent
> at night, conducted alternately by the chaplain and myself. At
> Tupelo, Miss., where I once requested Bishop Payne to preach
> for our command, General Forrest entertained him at his
> headquarters.[8]

After Bishop Payne preached, several of Forrest's officers
mingled with the bishop and, according to Kelley, one of
the men used profanity in front of the reverend, much to
Forrest's chagrin. Forrest pulled Kelley aside and offered to
"kick that hog out of the tent" if he deemed it so.[9]

Kelley recounts another time in which some of his men
captured a Union chaplain and brought him back to the
camp as a prisoner. The chaplain was terrified to learn that he
was going to be taken before the notorious Nathan Bedford
Forrest, but he found himself pleasantly surprised. Forrest
let the chaplain dine at his table and before eating asked
him to say the blessing. The stunned chaplain obliged and
cautiously ate his dinner. The next day Forrest personally
escorted the chaplain out of the camp, assuring him that he
had no fight against noncombatants like the minister. Forrest
even offered a little comic relief, telling the chaplain upon
his release, "Parson, I would keep you here to preach for me
if you were not needed so much more by the sinners on the
other side."[10]

As Forrest and Kelley sat mounted on their horses, watching
Fort Donelson get bombarded on that snowy February night
in 1862, Forrest suddenly sought divine intervention for the
salvation of the fort. He yelled at Kelley over the roars of
cannon fire and exhorted his captain: "Parson! For God's
sake pray! Nothing but God Almighty can save that fort!"[11]

At this time in his life, Forrest was a believer in the facts of Christianity but he as of yet did not have a true relationship with Christ. In the gospel of John, Jesus speaks with a Jewish Pharisee named Nicodemus, who seeks to know how one can enter the kingdom of Heaven. Jesus responds with the famous statement that sinners must be "born again."

> Truly, truly, I say to you, unless one is born of water and the Spirit he cannot enter into the kingdom of God. That which is born of the flesh is flesh, and that which is born of the Spirit is spirit. Do not be amazed that I said to you, 'You must be born again.' The wind blows where it wishes and you hear the sound of it, but do not know where it comes from and where it is going; so is everyone who is born of the Spirit. (John 3:5-8 NASB)

Being a respecter of Christ does not make one a partaker of Christ, and at this point Bedford was still not "born again," regardless of the respect he had towards Christians.

Meanwhile back at the fort, Generals John B. Floyd, Simon Buckner, and Gideon Pillow discussed plans to surrender. Floyd, the ranking officer in command, feared capture by the Union since he had recently served as secretary of war under Pres. James Buchanan and assumed he would be hanged as a traitor. Likewise, Pillow feared capture so he passed the buck to Buckner, who accepted it, offering to surrender the fort after the other two had safely escaped. Buckner, being an old friend of Grant's, suspected that at the very least he would escape with his life.

But Bedford Forrest had no plans to surrender. While the generals hypothesized about the massive amounts of reinforcements Grant had received, Forrest argued that their estimates were highly exaggerated. He had scouted the area and knew that the number of reinforcements was not as high as they originally had thought. He believed they could fight and save the fort. Nevertheless, he was outvoted and plans were made for surrender. Forrest angrily retorted that he did not come out to fight so that he could surrender his command and asked for permission to take his cavalry and "cut his way out." Permission was granted, and Forrest took to cutting. Under cover of nightfall he crossed a swollen ford and led his five hundred men to safety. It was his belief at the time that the infantry could have escaped also, but it was not to be. Ironically, some of the Confederates who surrendered at Donelson would join the Union army and meet up with Forrest again two years later at Fort Pillow. But there were many battles to be fought, and the next major engagement for Forrest and his men would be near a small Tennessee church, at a place called Shiloh.

Shiloh

It has been said that the Battle of Shiloh changed the war's outlook for both sides. Shiloh was a slaughterhouse that saw over twenty-three thousand men killed or wounded in the two-day struggle, which was more than all the casualties in every previous American war combined. It was here that the country first realized that this affair would be long and bloody, though none could have guessed how long and bloody it would become with over half a million killed in a four-year span. Many shots were fired at Shiloh, but the last bullet of the famous battle landed near the spine of Nathan Bedford Forrest.

The Federals were stunned when the Confederates launched their initial attack at Shiloh on April 6, 1862. Nevertheless they fought hard and casualties were high for both sides. Confederate general P. G. T. Beauregard wired Richmond that he expected to victoriously complete the battle the next day. Beauregard believed he had superior numbers and he had Ulysses S. Grant's army right where he wanted them. But that was about to change.

As night fell on April 6, Forrest and his men were ordered to a grove of trees to remain until daybreak. From there, he could overhear the Yankees talking and could witness the Federal reinforcements, seventeen thousand strong, of Union general Don Carlos Buell coming by boat up the river.

He headed off into the night to try and find Beauregard to warn that if they did not attack the Yankees under cover of darkness, they would be grossly outnumbered come morning. Unable to locate Beauregard, he went from camp to camp trying to find a higher-ranking officer who would listen. He eventually located Maj. Gen. William J. Hardee, but Forrest's admonition fell on deaf ears, and he was told that it was too late to change any battle plans. Forrest complained that unless they did something that night, they would be "whipped like Hell come morning."

As predicted, the next day saw a Confederate slaughter. After several hours of fierce fighting, the Southern infantry had to make a steady retreat towards the Mississippi border, with Forrest's cavalry providing cover for them.

Several miles from the battlefield, at a place called Fallen Timbers, Union general William Tecumseh Sherman's infantry pressed the Confederates until a small group of bold Southern cavalry charged the Yankees. Noticing that the Union infantry had become separated and disjointed in their advance, Forrest ordered a shocking, full-speed charge. Sherman was stunned, and his men were terrified. Many of them began an all-out retreat as Sherman lambasted them for their cowardice. As the Union infantry retreated they encountered some Union cavalry who assumed a massive Confederate force was approaching and joined in the retreat. Sherman was livid to see this many of his men running in the face of a mere 350 cavalry troops. At the head of the cavalry causing all of the commotion was Bedford Forrest. With his face flushed red and eyes blazing while he screamed a piercing rebel yell of "Charge!", Forrest drove the Yankees back.

Eventually, Forrest outran his men and found himself surrounded by Union soldiers. As he feverishly fought them off, they began yelling, "Kill him! Kill the Rebel! Knock him off his horse!" and Forrest took a gun blast to the side. Though it lifted him off his saddle, he was able to stay mounted and turn back towards his line. He then reached down and grabbed an unsuspecting Yankee soldier by the coat and swept him up onto his horse to ride on the rear, thus shielding himself from enemy fire. The Yankees held their fire, not wanting to kill one of their own, and in so doing allowed Forrest, now christened by many "the Wizard of the Saddle," to escape.

Once he was out of shooting range, Forrest dumped the Yankee on the ground, unharmed, and continued his flight back to camp. The wound he received was painful but not mortal, the bullet having come to rest less than an inch from his spine. Again the hand of God had graciously protected the daring warrior who could and probably should have lost his life at Shiloh.

Having tasted a fair amount of combat, Nathan Bedford Forrest found that he was a good soldier and to some extent may have even enjoyed the thrills of battle. He continued to recruit new volunteers for his cavalry, but the wording of his newspaper advertisements took on a more jocular tone, as evidenced by the following ad in the *Memphis Appeal*:

200 RECRUITS WANTED!

I will receive 200 able-bodied men if they will present themselves at my headquarters by the first of June with good horse and gun. I wish none but those who desire to be actively engaged. My headquarters for the present is at Corinth, Miss. Come on boys, if you want a heap of fun and to kill some Yankees.

N.B. Forrest, Colonel, Commanding
Forrest's Regiment[12]

It is interesting to note that Forrest's idea of fun had already nearly cost him his life several times and had almost left him paralyzed from his wound at Shiloh. As one Forrest biographer notes, "He was either a man who wanted to deceive his prospective recruits into thinking 'killing some Yankees' was going to be a 'heap of fun' or a man who actually felt it was."[13]

Murfreesboro

If the young lass Forrest encountered at Sacramento inspired him to "knightly chivalry," what happened at Murfreesboro would only add to his reputation as a rescuer of damsels in distress and a fierce defender of his people.

While riding towards Nashville, Forrest and his men came upon the small village of Woodbury, where they were greeted by a town full of hysterical women. The ladies reported that all the men in town had been arrested as Southern sympathizers and were now imprisoned just a few miles away at Murfreesboro. As if that was not bad enough, the women proceeded to tell how the local Federal marshal had forbidden them to meet in groups of more than three, even going so far as to prevent them from having church services. The murder of a Federal trooper in the area had apparently heightened tensions and led to numerous arrests, including that of William Owens, a local Baptist minister. Several of the men, including Owens, were sentenced to be hanged the next day. Forrest was sympathetic and incensed. He promised the women they would have their men back by sunset of the next day, and he set off with his men for Murfreesboro.

Meanwhile, at the jail, the men awaited their scheduled doom while Reverend Owens bowed on the cell floor, praying for deliverance. To the other prisoners, Owens' faithfulness must have appeared foolish. It seemed their fate was sealed, and all the praying in the world would not change that. Undeterred, Owens prayed on. Suddenly, around 4:30 in the morning, while the sun was still down, some of the prisoners heard a low rumble growing louder and louder and louder. At first they thought a thunderstorm was approaching. Then they discovered that Forrest and his cavalry were on their way.[14]

As part one of his plan, Bedford dispatched a portion of his men to capture the Federals keeping watch at the outskirts of town. Forrest's men masqueraded as Federal troops sent to relieve the others from picket duty then stealthily pulled their guns, capturing all fifteen Yankees without firing a shot. Step two involved sending another detachment to storm the jail and the courthouse, while a third group battled with infantry and cavalry troops in town. A mile outside of town another Union infantry regiment, plus four artillery guns, waited.

The scheme caught the Federals completely off guard, but many of them scurried to their guns and fought valiantly. Others ran and hid. The guards at the jail fired a few random shots at the prisoners, then set the building on fire before fleeing, but Forrest's men were able to pull them to safety before the building went up in smoke. As this was going on, Forrest himself rode up to get a report of how things were transpiring. With the characteristic fire in his eyes, an intense Forrest was told that the prison guard had set the jail on fire and escaped to the courthouse. Forrest vowed to catch him and eventually the guard was apprehended along with the remaining Federal troops. Having convinced the Federals of his overwhelming presence, Forrest dealt with the two remaining groups—the infantry outside of town and the infantry and cavalry in town— separately, calling each group to either surrender or be put to the sword. Already aware of and no doubt intimidated by Forrest's reputation, both groups surrendered and a grateful Murfreesboro fell back into Confederate hands, and the ladies of Woodbury received back their men.

In the fall of 1862, Bedford Forrest was assigned a new chief of artillery, nineteen-year-old John Morton, who had been captured at Fort Donelson and subsequently exchanged for Union prisoners. Morton had admired Forrest's daring escape from Donelson and sought to serve under him, sending a formal request to Gen. Braxton Bragg. The situation between Bragg and Forrest was already tense and would eventually explode a year later at Chickamauga, so the idea of Forrest exchanging his trusted artilleryman, Capt. Sam Freeman, for what he called a "tallow-faced boy" did not sit well with him. When Morton reported to his new chief, Forrest exploded and "without warning . . . cut loose with a barrage of profanity that stunned the red-cheeked Morton."[15] Ultimately, Forrest was allowed to keep both Freeman and Morton.

Eventually, he would change his opinion of Morton, who would prove to be one of his most faithful and fearless subordinates. While Forrest originally called him a "tallow-faced boy," he later referred to him as "the little kid with the big backbone." In fact a father-son bond would develop between the two men that extended beyond the Civil War until Forrest's death. Ironically, it was Morton who reportedly initiated Forrest into the Ku Klux Klan in 1868. And it was Morton who would write one of the earlier biographies of Forrest with his book *The Artillery of Nathan Bedford Forrest's Cavalry,* originally published in the 1890s. The boy would prove himself a man in battle, earning his general's respect by serving with him until the end of the war.

Parker's Crossroads

In December 1862, at the Battle of Parker's Crossroads, Bedford Forrest, now a brigadier general, would once again solidify his name in the annals of mounted warfare. Forrest and his men were ordered to destroy the rail lines in Western Tennessee that were supplying Union general Ulysses S. Grant at Vicksburg, Mississippi. While scouting the area, a detachment of men under Bedford's brother, Capt. Bill Forrest, spotted a Federal force estimated at ten thousand soldiers heading towards them. Union general Jeremiah Sullivan had wired Grant that he had Forrest in his sights but that the Confederate general had eight thousand mounted men with him. In reality, Forrest had about eighteen hundred, making him grossly outnumbered for the battle that would soon transpire. But Sullivan had good reason to overestimate Forrest's troop strength. As Forrest biographers Eddy Davison and Daniel Foxx write:

> Realizing that the enemy was very likely close enough for their spies to observe his camps, Forrest ordered dozens of campfires

built over a large area to simulate a huge force in bivouac. Small groups of troopers beat upon drums and barked commands to phantom companies, details of mounted troopers rode back and forth across the bridges, sometimes pulling the same pieces of artillery. The cavalrymen would then dismount, hide their horses, and become infantry, marching over the same bridges. He also had several Union sympathizers held prisoner who were allowed to see some of the demonstrations. Then, "out of the kindness of his heart," Forrest allowed them to escape and report whatever they believed their eyes to have beheld in the Confederate camps. Such deception was just another weapon to Forrest, and his men learned such tactics well, often using in their commander's absence the same tricks that made him so successful.[16]

Forrest's men converged with an eighteen-hundred-man regiment of Federals under Col. Cyrus Dunham at Parker's Crossroads, where the fighting commenced. It was here that Forrest displayed an oddball military tactic that proved to be ingenious. He had his artillery lead the foot troops into battle, seeking to leave his horses out of the fray. As Morton and Freeman maneuvered their guns, a sergeant named Nat Baxter began shifting towards the rear to find a better point from which to fire. Forrest mistook his act for an unordered retreat and whopped Baxter on the back with the smooth edge of his sword, bellowing, "Turn those horses around and get back where you belong or by God, I'll kill you."[17] Baxter explained what he was doing and Forrest relented. After the battle was over, feeling remorseful for his outburst, Forrest publicly commended the valor of his artillery, specifically mentioning Baxter for commendation.

With Forrest's artillery battering Dunham, things looked promising for the Confederates. So promising, in fact, that the two sides were discussing a surrender under a flag of truce when Forrest was suddenly stunned from behind. Two Union brigades under Col. John Fuller had attacked their rear and drastically turned the tables of the battle. As author and historian Shelby Foote wrote, "For the first, last, and only time in his career, Forrest was completely surprised in battle."[18] Forrest and his men were now trapped front and back by Federal troops. Riding to the rear to ascertain the situation, Forrest rode right into a nest of Union troops, who immediately demanded his surrender. He calmly informed them that he already had surrendered and stated that he would turn around and gather his "few remaining men," who would give up their arms. But surrender was not on Forrest's mind; another trick was. He thundered back towards his men, leaving the gullible Yankees dumbfounded.

Nevertheless, the situation had now become dire for the Confederates. It was at this time that one of his men, seeing the peril of their position, asked Forrest what, if anything, they could do. His reply to the question further solidified his legendary prowess and courage. "Split in two and charge both ways!" was his response. Though it has been disputed whether or not he actually uttered those words, they would be in keeping with his attitude under fire. As he had proven at Fort Donelson, he was much more likely to risk death and injury than he was to surrender, and somehow, some way, Forrest managed to fight his way out of the trap at Parker's Crossroads. He had once again narrowly escaped capture, and his fame would continue to spread.

Chapter 4

Forrest at War: 1863-1864

"All of them are wielders of the sword, expert in war; each man has his sword at his side, guarding against the terrors of the night." (Song of Solomon 3:8 NASB)

Nathan Bedford Forrest may have been a fierce and courageous warrior, but he was no fool. When his commanding officer, the twenty-six-year-old West Pointer Joseph Wheeler, began making plans for another assault on Fort Donelson, near Dover, Tennessee, Forrest balked. His men, woefully undersupplied and ragged, were in receipt of orders to attack a fortress that now stood a hundred miles into enemy territory, with no strategic advantage to achieve, even with victory. The best they could hope for was repossession of a useless fort, attained at the risk of losing many valuable men. Forrest aired his complaint to Wheeler, who disregarded it, ordering the battle to commence. Forrest obeyed with reservation, telling three of his staff officers that if he died in battle he wanted it known that he had opposed the action from the start.

The assault was a debacle for the South. Twice Forrest's cavalry was rebuffed when trying to charge the fort and twice Forrest had horses shot out from under him. That night while camped in a cabin, General Wheeler worked on his official report while Forrest sat nearby nursing his wounds. Wheeler, young enough to be Forrest's son, had gone against wise counsel and thus cost the lives of many. Forrest laid the primary blame at Wheeler's feet and would boldly tell him as much. As Wheeler dictated his report to a subordinate,

Forrest abruptly interrupted, saying, "I have no fault to find with my men. In both charges they did their duty as they have always done." Wheeler graciously responded that his report said nothing negative about Forrest or his men. But a livid Forrest continued:

> General Wheeler, I advised against this attack and said all a subordinate officer should have said against it, and nothing you can now say or do will bring back my brave men lying dead or wounded and freezing around that fort tonight. I mean no disrespect to you; you know my feelings of personal friendship for you; you can have my sword if you demand it; but there is one thing I do want you to put in that report to General Bragg—tell him that I will be in my coffin before I will fight again under your command.[1]

Though young, Wheeler showed tact beyond his years as he refused Forrest's offer of resignation and told him that as the commanding officer he took full responsibility for the defeat. He then honored Forrest's request and had him transferred out of his immediate command.

It was about this same time that God once again used one of his servants to touch Bedford Forrest's heart. James Larkins was a ninety-year-old farmer who lived near Dickson, Tennessee. Like many Southerners, he had been a proud Union man, but after Lincoln's call to raise seventy-five thousand volunteers to squelch the Confederacy, he had a change of heart. By the time the war began he had devoted himself and several of his grandsons to the Southern cause. The Larkins were devout Cumberland Presbyterians, and several of the men in the family had entered the ministry.[2] James' grandson and namesake, James Hugh McNeilly, graduated from seminary in 1856, was licensed as a Presbyterian minister in 1860, and volunteered to serve as a chaplain with the Forty-Ninth Tennessee Infantry, faithfully serving until the end of the war.[3] One of Larkins' other grandsons was killed at the Battle of Franklin in 1864, but the

Confederate cavalry general and West Point graduate Joseph Wheeler. Forrest served under Wheeler before a disagreement between the two led Forrest to vow never to serve under Wheeler again. By the end of Forrest's life they were on friendly terms again. (United States Library of Congress)

grandfather would not live to see that day. He did, however, live to see many Southern victories, and on one night in particular, he aided the Confederate cause by housing General Forrest and his staff.

By the time the war began, James Larkins had almost completely lost his eyesight, but not his spirit, nor his spunk. He kept his rifle with him at all times, just in case it was needed, and offered to aid the Confederates in any way he could. On his way back to Fort Donelson, Forrest and his men camped at the Larkins farm, spending the night with the elderly patriot. The next morning, James Larkins insisted on seeing the general off, and with the help of a family member, he walked Forrest to the road. While Forrest's staff rode on, the general stopped for a moment to say goodbye and express his gratitude to Larkins for his hospitality. It was then that the spirit of God moved in Larkins' heart, prompting him to perform an act that deeply affected Forrest. Larkins asked Forrest to get off his horse and kneel on the ground next to him so that he could pray for him. Forrest dutifully obliged, and the elderly man placed his hands on the general's head, turned his blind eyes toward Heaven, and interceded on behalf of Forrest, his men, and their cause.

Maybe the prayers reminded Forrest of the prayers he had heard his mother utter when he was a child. Maybe they reminded him of the prayers he had heard his wife say on his behalf numerous times over the years. Maybe the prayers reminded him that there was a greater spiritual battle being waged in his heart and that ultimately victory on the battlefield would mean little if he lost his soul. We do not know exactly what Nathan Bedford Forrest was thinking when James Larkins laid his hands on his head and interceded on his behalf. But when the general remounted his horse to ride off towards his next battle, his face was "bathed in tears."[4] Clearly God was working in Bedford Forrest's heart, and the Holy Spirit would continue to draw and convict him.

Make no mistake about it, Forrest believed the tenets

of Christianity. He never doubted that they were true; they just did not govern his life or his heart as they should have. The apostle Paul wrote to the Corinthian church, "I planted, Apollos watered, but God was causing the growth" (1 Corinthians 3:6 NASB). What was true in Biblical times was also true in the life of Nathan Bedford Forrest—and anyone who comes to faith in Christ. God uses many people in the process of drawing us to him. Mariam Forrest planted the seeds of faith in her son as he grew. Mary Ann Forrest tended those seeds by her stellar Christian witness, faithful testimony, and unending prayers. Now the aged James Larkins had sprayed the hardened heart of Bedford Forrest with spiritual water, and his prayer was already having profound effects on the general. In due time, God would supply the spiritual harvest, but for now Forrest would seek to redeem himself and his men on the field of battle.

Thompson's Station, Brentwood, and Franklin

Forrest sought redemption for his men and revenge against the Yankees who skewered them at Dover, and his revenge was achieved on March 4 at Thompson's Station. Under the command of Gen. Earl Van Dorn, another superior whom Forrest would clash with, the Confederates won a hard-earned victory as Forrest led a flank attack that trapped the Yankees and forced their surrender.

Apparently the loyalty Forrest was able to garner from his men also extended to his horses. One of his favorite mounts, Roderick, was wounded at the Battle of Thompson's Station, and Forrest immediately dismounted, sending the horse to the rear with his son, William. However, hearing the next round of volleys, Roderick broke loose and contrary to a horse's nature, ran towards the firing, seeking his master. Roderick was known to follow Forrest around camp like a pet dog, showing unusual loyalty and love for the general, but in seeking to be reunited with him, Roderick took yet another shot, this one fatal. He died on the battlefield just a few feet away from the warrior he faithfully followed. It was said of another one of Forrest's favorite mounts, named King Philip, that even after the war was over he would charge ferociously towards anyone he saw wearing the blue uniform of a Federal soldier. From boyhood, Bedford Forrest loved horses, and they always seemed to love him back, even when it sacrificially cost them their lives, as was the case with Roderick.

Forrest's next assignment would be to take his men and capture a five-hundred-troop Union detachment near Brentwood. In typical Forrest fashion, he flanked the Federals, hemming them in on all sides while carefully making sure there would be no surprises from behind like the one at Parker's Crossroads. He then demanded an immediate and unconditional surrender, dispatching Maj. Charles Anderson with a message to Union colonel Edward Bloodgood that they were "completely surrounded" and that if they did not surrender, he would "blow hell out of them in five minutes and won't take one of them alive if I have to sacrifice my men in storming their stockade."[5] Bloodgood either feigned courage or thought Forrest was bluffing, initially responding that Forrest would have to "come and get him." But a mere thirty minutes later, after witnessing Forrest's artillery moving into position, he had a change of heart and promptly surrendered all of his men.

It was this all-or-nothing demand for surrender that gained Forrest such a reputation for being a savage, take-no-prisoners type of warrior. But he was by no means the only commander to make such threats during the Civil War. Union general and ultimate hero Ulysses S. Grant gained notoriety and the nickname "Unconditional Surrender" for his hard-line approach to truces. William Tecumseh Sherman was known as a "butcher" and despised by many Southerners for his "total war" March to the Sea with his infamous promise to "make Georgia howl," which he followed with a torching of South Carolina to punish them for being the first state to secede. Even the saintly and pious Gen. Thomas "Stonewall" Jackson advocated a "black flag" strategy of killing as many Yankees as possible, as quickly as possible, in order to force a Union surrender and more quickly end the war. In Forrest's case, the ultimate desire was to capture a fort without having to resort to bloodshed. And in his mind, once the ultimatum was made, the Yankees had no one to blame but themselves if they were slaughtered since they had rebuffed their chance to peacefully surrender. If they chose to fight, then in his mind, they were choosing death and therefore deserved it when it was inflicted upon them.

Though we usually divide the armies of the Civil War along North-South lines, in many ways it is the east-west division that proved to be more decisive in battle. The east was made up of fierce fighters, but many of them were more aristocratic in their approach, oftentimes fighting a British-style "gentleman's war." But westerners, like Forrest, who grew up on the Tennessee frontier, and Grant, from Illinois, tended to see war as a fight unto death, with nothing gentlemanly about it. Forrest was famous for saying, "War means fightin' and fightin' means killin'"—but this is much more than just a pithy musing from a backwoods farmer. This was his true philosophy of war. The point was not to be respected by the enemy, the point was to be victorious over the enemy. Southern men like Forrest and Jackson saw the Yankees as invaders who deserved what they got. Modern pacifistic ears may find that appalling, but Forrest was not concerned with what people thought of him. Victory was what mattered; and victory would only be attained by the enemy's surrender—or death.

Sometimes, however, the death came to Forrest's men rather than the enemy. This was the case a few weeks later at Franklin, Tennessee, where the Confederates won a victory, but Forrest lost one of his best men. Artillery captain Sam Freeman was captured at Franklin and subsequently shot in the head after surrendering. Though Forrest is well known due to the alleged massacre at Fort Pillow, he was at times on the receiving end of atrocities, as Freeman's death proves. Forrest was deeply saddened at losing the popular Freeman. Riding up to the body, he dismounted and knelt next to the artillery captain, taking the dead man's hand. He fought back tears as he quietly said, "Brave man. None braver."[6]

Sand Mountain

Shortly after this, Forrest was off on his next adventure, which entailed tracking down Union colonel Abel Streight, who had been assigned the task of forging deep into the Confederacy and raiding Bragg's supply lines. Knowing he would encounter some rough mountain country, Streight had the unusual idea of using mules rather than horses for his cavalry. His plan got off to a rocky start when several of the mules he received by requisition proved unsuitable for such a journey, and the ones that were able to make the trip were too ornery to ride. Eventually he got the mules and his men organized and headed for northern Alabama, where he would be stalked by Forrest and his men.

The two armies skirmished at Sand Mountain and across Alabama, moving east towards Georgia, with Forrest slowly getting the upper hand on Streight and his "mule brigade" until they reached a place called Black Creek. It was here that Streight's men managed to cross a bridge then set it on fire before the Confederates could catch up. Forrest had already sent a message ahead to the residents of Rome, Georgia, warning them of the Federals' approach, and now it appeared that Streight's men would escape the grasp of the dreaded Forrest cavalry.

Enter Emma Sansom. Sixteen-year-old Emma Sansom had watched the events transpire and ran up to Forrest, promising to show him a shallow spot in the creek where his men could cross. She asked for someone to quickly saddle her horse so she could show them, but Forrest said there was not time for that. He put her on the back of his horse and promised her worried mother: "Don't be uneasy; I will bring her back safe."[7]

A short while later Sansom was safely back at home and Forrest's men were across the creek in hot pursuit. The chase ended a few miles from Rome when Streight's men and mules were forced to stop out of sheer exhaustion. As they made their battle line, several of the boys in blue fell asleep, even as the Confederates were firing at them. Forrest knew they were physically whipped, just as his own troops were severely fatigued, so he sought to end the battle by employing one of his common ruses. Under a flag of truce, he met with Colonel Streight to discuss surrender. Initially, Forrest gave lenient terms, offering to allow the Federal officers to keep their side arms and personal property, but Streight would not bite. So, within sight of the Union officer, Forrest had his artillery guns brought past repeatedly to give the impression that they had more than they did. As Forrest spoke to Streight, the colonel distractedly looked over Forrest's shoulder, counting Confederate artillery pieces as they passed. "How many guns have you got? There's fifteen I've counted already," Streight queried. Forrest replied, "I reckon that's all that has kept up. But I've got enough to whip you out of your boots."[8] Furthermore, Forrest had subordinates ride up to him while he was talking with Streight, saying that yet another regiment had arrived and the field was getting crowded. The ruse finally ended when Forrest turned while still talking with Streight and bellowed out to one of his men to prepare the cavalry to mount and charge. Streight finally folded. He surrendered his eighteen hundred men to Forrest's four hundred, and only after surrendering did he find out that Forrest was bluffing. He immediately demanded to have his guns back so they could "fight it out." But Forrest just laughed at him and said, "You know what they say Colonel . . . all's fair in love and war!"[9]

Shortly after the battle with Abel Streight, an incident involving Forrest occurred that reminded everyone that the general was not one to be trifled with and could be deadly when cornered. In fighting with Streight's men near Sand

Mountain, the Confederates had lost two artillery guns. Lt. Andrew Gould had given the order to abandon the equipment since, in his opinion, it would be impossible to keep it and retreat without heavy casualties. When Forrest learned of it he was infuriated, determining that the loss of equipment was due to Gould's cowardice, and decided to have the lieutenant transferred out of his command and replaced with an abler and braver man. Gould was highly insulted by the claims and insisted that Forrest either rescind the transfer request or at least exonerate him in the wording of it. Forrest adamantly refused, and a confrontation loomed.

Artillery commander John Morton, who was friendly with both men, tried to act as mediator, but to no avail. Morton knew that both men were hot tempered and violent and that if they met blood would surely spill. On June 13, 1863, at the Masonic building in Columbus, Tennessee, Morton's greatest fears were realized. The best witnesses to what happened were a group of four young boys who had followed Forrest into the building to catch a glimpse of the famed general. While Forrest stood in an office visiting with his quartermaster, an irate Gould appeared and asked to speak with him. Forrest folded up a penknife that he had been whittling with and placed it in his pocket. He then joined Gould in the hallway, where the conversation quickly grew heated. Gould made his demands, and Forrest refused. As both men became more agitated, Gould made a move towards a pistol in his pocket. When he did, Forrest reached out and grabbed him with his right hand, slipping his left hand into his pocket to retrieve his penknife. Forrest stealthily opened the knife with his teeth and thrust it into Gould's side just as the lieutenant's pistol went off, shooting through his pocket and wounding Forrest right above his hip.

Gould ran and a livid Forrest followed. Several officers appeared after hearing the commotion and convinced the general to be examined by a nearby doctor. Working feverishly in an intense environment, the doctor initially stated that he believed the wound to Forrest would prove fatal. At that, Forrest exploded, leaping from the table and pursuing Gould once more, bellowing, "No damned man shall kill me and live!"

Forrest stumbled into the street, pulled a gun from a nearby saddlebag, and began searching for Gould. One man ran up to him and told him the wound to Gould was fatal, so he should give up pursuit, but another man claimed that the wound was not severe at all, and he pointed to a tailor shop where Gould had gone for care. Forrest entered the shop enraged; as he did, Gould slid from the table on which he was being examined and fled through the back alley. Forrest fired but missed his intended target, instead slightly wounding a bystander in the leg. Finally, Forrest caught up to his quarry, who was lying in some tall grass. Forrest walked up, determined that Gould was near death, and left him there.

The doctors who had been attending to Gould now attended to Forrest, who was ushered back to his hotel room, where his wife and son were waiting. When he saw Mary Ann, he immediately calmed down and cleaned up his language, once more submitting to a doctor's examination. With a more detailed observation of the wound, the doctor determined that the ball had landed in muscle, rather than intestine, and that Forrest would be fine in a couple of days. Upon hearing this, the general sent the men to care for Gould and to do all they could to save him. Forrest joked that if Gould had acted with such bravery in battle the incident would have never occurred in the first place.

According to some reports, Forrest made amends with Gould while the latter was on his deathbed. Gould died shortly thereafter as a fatal example of what Forrest was capable of when provoked. Though the incident was clearly a case of self-defense, it proved how deadly Forrest could be—a lesson that many of the bystanders quickly learned and never forgot.

Chickamauga

In September 1863, Forrest was involved in a major engagement near Chattanooga, Tennessee, at a place called Chickamauga Creek. Forrest's commander was a West Point graduate, Gen. Braxton Bragg, who had become extremely unpopular with many of his subordinates, including Forrest. Bragg was thought by many to be an inferior commander due to his nervous anxiety and inability to stay the course once a plan of action was established. Fickle and indecisive, Bragg in large part had lost the confidence of his men by the time Chickamauga commenced.

Bragg also had a habit of always finding scapegoats to blame when battles did not turn out as expected. Add to this a mercurial temper that could fire slanderous barbs at those who opposed him, and it is easy to see why he was not highly esteemed by his men. Unfortunately, he was a favorite of Confederate president Jefferson Davis. A West Point classmate and longtime friend, Davis defended Bragg and kept him in high levels of command, much to the chagrin of many in the Southern army. Bragg's unpopularity reached its apex when many of his immediate subordinates sent a formal letter to Davis asking for Bragg to be relieved of command.

Leonidas Polk, a general under Bragg and also a close friend of Davis's, described Bragg as "a poor, feeble-minded irresolute man of violent passions . . . uncertain of the soundness of his conclusions and therefore timid in their executions."[10] Generals William Hardee, Patrick Cleburne, and Benjamin Cheatham all sought his removal, preferring to have the more congenial and confident Joseph Johnston named commander. William Gale, a member of Polk's staff, described Bragg as "obstinate . . . ruthless without enterprise, crafty yet without stratagem, suspicious, envious, jealous, vain, a bantam in success and a dunghill in disaster."[11] Forrest would soon be added to the list of Bragg detractors, and not surprisingly, he would have a very public and volatile encounter with his superior, which came to a head shortly after Chickamauga.

Gen. Braxton Bragg. Forrest would serve under Bragg at the Battle of Chickamauga, where Bragg's indecisiveness led to Forrest's unleashing a tirade upon the commander. Forrest demanded a transfer and was granted it. (United States Library of Congress)

Technically, Chickamauga was a Confederate victory as Bragg's army, with Polk, Cheatham, John Bell Hood, and James Longstreet, along with Forrest and Joseph Wheeler commanding cavalry, forced the Union army under William S. Rosecrans into a retreat towards Chattanooga. In spite of the Confederate victory, causalities were high for both sides, and in many eyes, the South lost a chance for a much greater victory. Lines of communication were mixed up, and many of Bragg's subordinates did not initially receive orders from him. When they finally did receive them, they commenced with the battle plan, but it was much later in the day than hoped for. Once the Federals began their retreat, many of the Confederates, including Forrest, sought to pursue them and crush the fleeing army. But, per his custom, Bragg hesitated.

Having personally scaled a tall tree just outside Chattanooga, Forrest witnessed with his own eyes the disorderly retreat of the Northern army and sensed a chance to move in for the kill. He sent information to his immediate commander, Polk, who pressed Bragg to no avail. After sending a few more dispatches to Bragg with requests for an advance, Forrest finally went to personally admonish Bragg to move. Bragg would not be budged. Exasperated, Forrest stormed away from Bragg's tent, exclaiming, "What does he fight battles for?"[12]

Shortly after the battle, Forrest received word that he was to hand his brigade over to Wheeler for a special expedition. Forrest grudgingly complied then took a ten-day furlough to LaGrange, Georgia, where he was reunited with his beloved wife. While there he received another dispatch from Bragg, saying that he was to report to Wheeler, who would now be his commanding officer. In Forrest's eyes this was the last straw. He had already butted heads with Wheeler before, swearing that he would never serve under him again. Now, already simmering from Bragg's order to hand over a group of cavalrymen that he himself had raised and supplied, Forrest decided to clear the air and "turn it blue" with a personal visit to Bragg's headquarters.

Accompanied by J. B. Cowan, his doctor and his wife's cousin, Forrest marched to Bragg's tent, stormed past the guard, and approached Bragg. When Bragg stood and extended his hand to Forrest, he slapped it away, then with his index finger repeatedly pointing in Bragg's face, unleashed a torrent of words that had been brewing for months. His famous temper running away from him, Forrest blasted Bragg:

> You commenced your cowardly and contemptible persecution of me soon after the battle of Shiloh, and you have kept it up ever since. . . . You robbed me of my command in Kentucky, and gave it to one of your favorites—men whom I armed and equipped from the enemies of our country. In a spirit of revenge and spite, because I would not fawn upon you as others did, you drove me into west Tennessee in the winter of 1862 with a second brigade I had organized, with improper arms and without sufficient ammunition, although I had made repeated applications for the same. You did it to ruin me and my career. When in spite of all this I returned well equipped by captures, you began again your work of spite and persecution, and have kept it up; and now this second brigade, organized and equipped without thanks to you or the government, a brigade which has won a reputation for successful fighting second to none in the army, taking advantage of your position as the commanding general in order to further humiliate me, you have taken these brave men from me. I have stood your meanness as long as I intend to. You have played the part of a damned scoundrel, and are a coward, and if you were any part of a man I would slap your jaws and force you to resent it. You may as well not issue any orders to me, for I will not obey them, and I will hold you personally responsible for any further indignities you endeavor to inflict upon me. You have threatened to arrest me for not obeying your orders promptly. I dare you to do it, and I say to you that if you ever again try to interfere with me or cross my path it will be at the peril of your life![13]

Bragg was shocked and Cowan was terrified, telling Forrest

as they walked off, "Well, you're in for it now!" But Forrest was unworried, answering, "He'll never say a word about it; he'll be the last man to mention it; and mark my word, he'll take no action in the matter. I will ask to be relieved and transferred to a different field, and he will not oppose it."[14]

Forrest's intuition proved to be right. While Forrest's actions were clearly insubordinate, nothing came of it. Bragg was known to have a temper himself, but he seems to have been thoroughly intimidated by Forrest's barrage and simply chose to seek his transfer rather than his court-martial. Forrest would have no further personal dealings with Braxton Bragg.

Okolona

Returning west, to Tennessee and Mississippi, Forrest came under the overall command of Joe Johnston and the immediate command of Stephen Dill Lee, who showed Forrest great deference and respect and who would remain a close friend even after the war. The military situation for Forrest was greatly improved, but the sacrifices of battle would hit him hard near Okolona, Mississippi.

Forrest once again needed to recruit troops, having only a handful of his most trusted subordinates, including his baby brother Jeffrey. Serving as a colonel under his older brother, Jeffrey was the youngest of the Forrest family, having been born four months after the death of their father, William. Consequently, Jeffrey became more of a son than a brother to the then sixteen-year-old Bedford. Bedford raised him from birth, and once he moved to Memphis and began amassing his fortune, Bedford sent for Jeffrey, whom he supported and had educated. Of all the Forrest brothers, many of whom served under Bedford, Jeffrey was clearly his favorite.

Near Okolona, Forrest's cavalry would engage the seven thousand men of Union general William Sooy Smith. Employing his customary moves of surprise flank attacks and full-speed charges, Forrest flummoxed Smith into a broken retreat with skirmishing all along the retreat line.

With Bedford and his brother Jeffrey both leading the way into a fierce enemy fire, tragedy struck. Bedford saw Jeffrey recoil and fall from his horse. Screaming, "Jeffrey! Jeffrey!" the general dismounted and ran to his brother, who had been shot in the throat. As Jeffrey lay dying, the final drops of blood trickling down him, Bedford held his head in his lap, repeatedly kissed his brow, and sobbed, crying over and over again, "Oh, Jeffrey! . . . Oh, Jeffrey! . . . Oh, Jeffrey!"

It was as though for a few moments time stopped on the battlefield. The Federals, exhausted and battle weary, ceased fire. The Confederates could only helplessly watch their bereaved general. His beloved Jeffrey was gone, but the battle and the war would have to go on. Forrest rose to his feet, wiped the tears from his eyes, placed a hat over his brother's face, gave orders for the care of his body, then commanded the bugler to sound the charge. Forrest, a man with a legendary temper, fighting skills, and bravery second to none, was set on vengeance. In an ear-piercing scream, he called his men to "Charge!" And they commenced, with Forrest leading the way.

His men thought him so grief-stricken that he was on a death march to join his brother. Within a short span of time, Forrest was able to catch up with the Federals and engage in a fierce battle of hand-to-hand fighting in which he was surrounded and outnumbered. He promptly killed three men before the remainder of his troops caught up with him. And when they did, they found their general violently attacking the enemy. His doctor and relative, J. B. Cowan, pleaded with him to return to the rear, where he would not be in such mortal danger, but Forrest refused, telling the doctor to go back himself if he was worried. At that very moment, Forrest's horse was shot from under him, but he commandeered another mount and pressed on.

In the heat of the fighting, Forrest and Cowan noticed a terrified woman and her children trying to find shelter amidst the carnage. "Forrest noted a hole in the ground where clay had been dug to build the chimney, and he sent Cowan over to lead them to that better refuge. 'In there,' he told Cowan. 'They will be perfectly safe.'"[15]

Forrest fought on, having a second horse shot from under him. The Federals decided to charge the outnumbered Confederates, and eventually another intense round of hand-to-hand combat ensued. Many of the men were now out of ammunition and without their horses, yet they fought on by throwing whatever objects they could find: empty pistols, rocks, and fists. Confederate major Thomas Tate almost lost his life when a Union officer leveled his pistol at point-blank range and prepared to fire. Just a moment before the trigger was squeezed, Forrest rode up and slashed at the Federal with his sword, partially decapitating him.

Yet even in the midst of the most violent battles, Forrest could show compassion for the helpless. As he rode upon a Union hospital that had been hastily abandoned in retreat, he came upon the gruesome scene of a Federal solider with a saw halfway through his leg, having been in the middle of an amputation when the doctor fled. Forrest ordered Dr. Cowan to administer chloroform and complete the surgery.

With his men exhausted and out of ammunition, Forrest finally gave up pursuit, and William Smith limped back over the Tennessee border with his Federal cavalry to rejoin the army of William Tecumseh Sherman.

Chapter 5

Fort Pillow: Forrest's Notorious Legacy

"For we know that the whole creation groans and suffers the pains of childbirth together until now." (Romans 8:22 NASB)

Typically, those who make the greatest impact upon society are people who are radically polarizing. Their fans rally to their side and defend them against all enemy assaults, while their detractors despise them with a blind rage. Clearly this is the case with Nathan Bedford Forrest, and nowhere can this reality be more evidently seen than in the assault and subsequent arguments surrounding Fort Pillow.

Fort Pillow was constructed by Confederate soldiers under the leadership of Gen. Gideon Pillow in 1862. Built on the banks of the Mississippi River, the horseshoe-shaped fort had three levels of earthen fortifications in front of the main wall and was open in the rear to the river. The fort changed hands a couple of times during the war before being abandoned and then eventually reoccupied by the Federals.

By March 1864 the atmosphere in Western Tennessee had become poisonous. Forrest and his men had liberated the town of Jackson from Federal rule and set up their temporary headquarters in the city. From the citizens they heard numerous accounts of atrocities committed under the leadership of Union cavalry colonel Fielding Hurst, head of the Sixth Tennessee Cavalry (U.S.A.). Hurst had a reputation for extorting money from Southerners by threatening to torch their towns if they did not comply with his wishes. It was determined that he had taken more than five thousand dollars from the citizens of Jackson by such dishonest means, and Forrest vowed to do something about it. Writing letters to his commanding officer, Leonidas Polk, as well as the Federal government, Forrest demanded that the citizens of Jackson be given restitution. The Federal government eventually agreed, though Hurst later reappeared in Jackson and bled the money from its residents once again.

Ironically, Forrest would graciously take extraordinary steps to prevent Hurst's home from being destroyed by angry Confederates. Near Hurst's hometown of Purdy, Tennessee, Forrest dispatched his chief of staff, Charles Anderson, along with five men, telling them to find Hurst's home and guard it against vandalism. When they came to the door, a terrified Mrs. Hurst answered, fully expecting to suffer for the wrongs of her husband. "Are you the wife of Colonel Hurst?" Anderson asked. "Yes sir," she replied. What Anderson said next, stunned her.

> We are not here to harm you, but have been sent for your protection. Although General Forrest has not reached Purdy, he is aware of the ruin and devastation caused by your husband's regiment, and has sent me in advance of his troops to place a guard around your house. This guard is from his own escort, and will remain with you until all of our command has passed, and I assure you that neither your family or anything about your premises will be disturbed or molested.

A grateful Mrs. Hurst responded, "Please, sir, say to General Forrest, for me, that this is more than I had any right to expect of him, and that I thank him from my heart for this unexpected kindness. I shall gratefully remember it and shall always believe him to be as generous as he is brave."[1]

Mrs. Hurst may have been appreciative, but Colonel Hurst was unaffected by the kindness. In addition to extortion, he was accused of holding citizens as prisoners without cause, a common occurrence during the Civil War. Forrest took particular offense to the case of a minister named G. W. D. Harris of Dyer County, Tennessee, who was being held at Fort Pillow. In correspondence to Federal general Ralph

Buckland, Forrest demanded that "Mr. Harris be granted a fair trail before a competent tribunal, or else unconditionally and promptly released, or otherwise I shall place in close confinement 5 Federal soldiers, now in my hands, as hostages for his protection, and in case he should die in your hands from ill treatment these men shall be duly executed in retaliation."[2]

While these accusations against Hurst were bad, the alleged atrocities got much worse. Forrest cited seven murders Hurst's men had committed against Tennesseans, including a case of torture and execution committed against Willis Dodds, a young soldier from Forrest's cavalry. Dodds was captured in Henderson County at the home of his father and was subsequently found hanging in a tree with his hands and feet bound and his face and genitals cut off. For all these crimes, Forrest demanded Hurst and any accomplices be handed over as prisoners to be duly tried by the Confederate States of America. Not surprisingly, the Federal government refused to comply.

By April 1864, Fort Pillow housed close to 600 Union soldiers, 253 of which were black men, many of whom were escaped slaves. Of the white men serving the fort, several were former Confederate soldiers who had deserted to the North, while others were the much maligned Tennessee Yankees, also known as Tennessee Tories, local men whose loyalties were with the North rather than the South. Needless to say, Fort Pillow was made up of men who did not have the respect of the Southern army or its citizenry.

The commander in charge was Maj. Lionel Booth, with the second in command being a notorious and hated Tennessee Yankee by the name of William Bradford. Booth was sent to Fort Pillow by his commanding officer, Gen. Stephen A. Hurlbut, headquartered at Memphis, because of concerns over Major Bradford's youth and inexperience. Time would prove that Hurlbut's fears were well founded.

The Civil War saw many political hacks who sought war heroism as a way of career advancement. By gaining an officer's commission they could perhaps get their names in the newspapers and gain fame because of the valor of the armies that served under them. The problem in many cases was that they had no military training or acumen. Sometimes a lack of training caused little if any problem, as evidenced by Forrest himself, who had almost no education yet possessed the natural instincts of a warrior. Other times, the lack of military training, or perhaps the simple lack of a military mind, proved catastrophic. Such would be the case with Bradford. A lawyer who hailed from the same Bedford County, Tennessee, of Forrest's birth, Bradford had made a name for himself through litigation and in the eyes of his fellow citizens, treachery. Fiercely loyal to the Union, he had attained a major's commission from the Federal government but gained nothing short of outright hatred from many of his fellow Tennesseans.

In March 1864, Forrest and his men raided strategic locations, capturing Federal soldiers as well as much needed supplies. At Paducah, Kentucky, during one such raid, Forrest had occupied the town while the 650 Union soldiers retreated to nearby Fort Anderson. The Confederates subsequently assaulted Fort Anderson, where Forrest issued what was becoming his normal surrender-or-die ultimatum. But unlike times in the past, this time his bluff may have been called; Union colonel Stephen Hicks refused to surrender. While there is some disagreement as to whether the Federals adequately repulsed Forrest or if he chose to leave of his own accord, the Confederate general left Paducah on March 25, heading back to Tennessee with supplies. Forrest claimed that he found small pox raging through Paducah, and so he abandoned the city for health reasons. Regardless of the reasons for leaving, one thing seems clear: Forrest's well-known fame for issuing ultimatums was beginning to be challenged by the Federals.

Fort Pillow, at least originally, was not very high on Forrest's priority list. Indeed, some said that it was a fairly harmless and worthless fort that he should not have concerned himself with, but some other factors convinced him otherwise. One factor was supplies. By this point, Forrest and his men were again in need of more horses, saddles, guns, and food, whatever they could gain from victories over the Federals. No doubt, by conquering Pillow, he would be able to add more provisions to his cavalry.

Another factor was the men who occupied Fort Pillow. The white Union troops under Bradford had earned a reputation for pillaging the Southern citizens of the area. Indeed, such civilian plundering was not uncommon by Union armies that deemed disloyalty to the Federal government to be treason and therefore felt justified in "confiscating" whatever personal property they chose to help themselves to. Reportedly, Forrest was "distressed by well-authenticated instances, repeatedly brought to his notice of rapine and atrocious outrages upon non-combatants of the country, by the garrison at Fort Pillow."[3] The Federals were also accused of "venting upon the wives and daughters of Southern soldiers the most opprobrious and obscene epithets, with more than one extreme outrage upon the persons of these victims of their hate and lust."[4] Clarke Barteau, who served as a colonel under Forrest, stated, "For days before the capture of Fort Pillow, citizens fleeing to us from its vicinity brought doleful tales of outrages committed by the Federal forces in that stronghold. The helpless families of some of our soldiers had been victims of their raiding parties. A strong feeling prevailed in favor of capturing the fort, but it was not expected to be done without fighting and loss of life."[5]

While the civilized rules of war dictated that noncombatants were not to be molested, this seldom held true in the Civil War South. Suspicions ran high, and loyalty was constantly questioned. Oaths were required, and high taxes levied against Southern citizens who were deemed to be sympathizers with the rebellion. In such an atmosphere, it is not hard to see how many in the South would view men like Nathan Bedford

Forrest as their so-called knight in shining armor. And its not hard to see how Forrest, his men, and the citizens of West Tennessee would view Bradford's Tennessee Yankees as villainous miscreants who were traitors to their own people and terrorists of the innocent. Such was the mindset of the times, and the bad blood between the Tennessee Yankees and the Wizard of the Saddle would soon come to a head.

Not only had Forrest and his men heard secondhand reports of Yankees plundering, many of his troops had experienced it personally as their families reported some of the atrocities taking place while the men were off fighting the war. Several times, citizens near Fort Pillow specifically requested that Forrest do something about the Union garrison there, and at least on one occasion, a delegation of citizens from Jackson, Tennessee, pleaded with Forrest to keep a detachment stationed in the area for protection. Initially, Forrest did not believe he had enough men to deal with the problem, but the tearful pleas by some of the ladies apparently changed his mind. According to Ted Brewer of the Twentieth Tennessee, "General Forrest was a man of great sympathy and when he heard the pathetic stories told by the ladies he changed his plans and decided to attack Fort Pillow. . . . Forrest felt that if he ignored the citizens' complaints he would lose many new recruits to desertion before he could reach northern Mississippi."[6]

This account seems plausible for at least two reasons. First, Forrest was always known to be sympathetic where ladies were concerned. He revered his mother and was close to his twin sister growing up. He also deeply respected his wife and was always careful to watch his language and mind his manners when she was present. Additionally, he wrote in his official record that the young girl who assisted him at the Battle of Sacramento had "infused him with knightly chivalry." Right or wrong, Forrest saw himself as a protector of Southern women, and when these tearful pleas came, he no doubt succumbed to their requests. The second reason

Brewer cited was more practical. If Forrest ignored the plight of these Tennesseans, he was sure to lose a certain amount of public support. Always in desperate need of new recruits, he knew he was more likely to get them by faithfully defending the citizens against Northern atrocities.

Because of these factors, Forrest decided to move on Fort Pillow. Yet even then he did not seem to regard the matter as a major battle concern. In a letter to commanding general Joseph Johnston, he mentioned, almost in passing, of a Union presence at Fort Pillow that he would "deal with in a couple of days." Indeed he would "deal with" them and what took place would dog him to his dying day.

On the morning of April 12, two Southern brigades under the command of Gen. James R. Chalmers surrounded the fort as Confederate sharpshooters picked off any Federal who dared raise his head above the parapets. Chalmers and his men made short order of the first two lines of earthwork pickets and were simply awaiting further instructions when Forrest came upon the scene at 10:00 A.M. Under heavy fire from the Federals, Forrest had two horses shot out from under him that morning, leaving him slightly injured. He dispatched sixteen hundred men under Colonels Robert McCulloch and Tyree Bell to storm the final earthwork, from where Federal sharpshooters were firing, and thus overwhelm them. Forrest then rode to the rear to be treated for his injury. Once the final level of earthworks were taken, the only thing left to do was obtain a surrender from the Yankees—or storm the fort and overwhelm the outnumbered Federals by force.

The only hope that the Federals had was the *New Era,* a Union gunboat that had been firing at Forrest's men from the river. Eventually seeing that they were having no effect, the vessel ceased fire and moved on. The *New Era*'s departure was a massive blow to the Federals' already fading chance of survival.

The other massive blow came that morning when Booth, the commanding officer in charge, was killed by a sharpshooter. This put the young and skittish Bradford in command, and in his inexperience, or perhaps arrogance, he failed to see that surrender was his only option. And surrender was requested by General Forrest—three times.

In typical fashion, Forrest sent a message to Booth (not knowing he was already dead), under a flag of truce:

> Major: your gallant defense of Fort Pillow has entitled you to the treatment of brave men. I now demand the unconditional surrender of your forces, at the same time assuring you that you will be treated as prisoners of war. I have received a new supply of ammunition and can take your works by assault, and if compelled to do so you must take the consequences.
>
> N.B. Forrest, Major General
> Commanding Confederate Cavalry[7]

Bradford wrote back requesting an hour to receive counsel from his officers as well as the officers manning the gunboats in the river. The problem was that Forrest's surrender request had nothing to do with the boats. He wrote back saying the surrender of the gunboats was not required. As for the fort, he would give them twenty minutes, rather than an hour, to decide their fate.

Mention of the gunboats also apparently raised Forrest's suspicions. He knew there were more boats in the area, so while the cease-fire was under effect, Forrest sent some men to monitor the river in case Federal reinforcements should arrive. Forrest suspected that Bradford's request of one hour was a stalling tactic to allow time for boatloads of new forces, and he was in no mood to allow that to happen. Bradford finally sent his message to Forrest, written in the name of the deceased Major Booth, stating that he would not surrender the fort. Now, the scene was set for catastrophe and behind the walls of the fort, the situation was becoming more dangerous.

While the flag of truce was waving, the men inside Fort Pillow began to rise up over the fortifications and taunt the Confederate army. As historian Jay Winik writes: "Not only did the fort commander refuse, but the cocky Federals openly taunted Forrest, daring him to try to take the garrison. It was the mistake of their lives."[8] This seems to be rather bizarre behavior for a troop of outnumbered men facing a general known to be one of the most skilled warriors on either side of the conflict. What could be the source of such false bravado? Were they unaware of the overwhelming numbers they faced? That would be hard to imagine since they had faced a hail of bullets raining down upon them every time they looked over the walls. Did they not realize that it was Nathan Bedford Forrest and his fierce and famous fighters who were assailing them? Again this seems unlikely since everyone knew Forrest was in the area and the communications coming from the Confederates had been written in his name. Such foolish taunting in the midst of overwhelming odds had to have a natural explanation, and indeed it did. The men of Fort Pillow had become bulletproof, at least in their own minds, as a result of numerous whiskey barrels that had been stationed at various spots around the fort to induce artificial courage. Alcohol was the last bit of kindling to be added to this smoldering fire, and the subsequent taunts further angered the Southern men, who really needed nothing else to inspire them to destroy the place. The results were devastating, controversial, and tragic on several levels.

Forrest ordered twelve hundred men to charge the fort while Confederate sharpshooters laid down a galling cover fire to the parapets. Once inside the fort, a chaotic melee ensued with point-blank shots being fired and hand-to-hand combat engaged in on mass levels. The Federals were completely outmanned, outgunned, and overpowered. Some retreated towards the Mississippi River, where they wrongly assumed Union boats would come to their aid. Others fought gallantly. Still others laid down arms, offering to surrender. Of these, some were taken prisoner while others were reportedly shot, being shown no quarter. In the midst of the chaos, according to the Confederates, some Federals would lay down their arms and surrender, only to run again, pick up a weapon, and fire. It was difficult to tell who had genuinely surrendered and who had not. All the while, the Union flag continued to wave over the fort, advertising to all who could see that the Federals had not surrendered and the fight was still on. As for Forrest, he was outside the fort until twenty minutes after the assault began.

Testimony of what occurred was varied and conflicting. As Davison and Foxx write, "The easy question: was there needless killing at Fort Pillow? There was. The difficult questions may never be put to rest. The one constant in such an investigation of controversial behavior on the battlefield is that armed conflict clouds judgment and loosens, even makes useless, the rules of civilized society."[9] For those who have never experienced combat, especially the hand-to-hand, close-quartered Civil War style, it is impossible to truly understand what goes on in a soldier's head and the actions that ensue. It is easy for the pacifist to kick back in his easy chair, in the safety of his living room, and cast judgment upon the man who wages war in the midst of a kill-or-be-killed struggle. Therefore all civilian commentators—this author included—who would offer their analysis would be wise to admit their limited perspective as it relates to combat conditions. In the midst of utter chaos, with bullets flying, swords slashing, bayonets being thrust, and punches being thrown, survival instincts kick in. Soldiers are not thinking about etiquette, they are thinking about living to fight another day. *Insanitas belli,* the fury of battle, has caused incidents in every war in history that make people pause and question the rightness or wrongness of such actions. But *insanitas belli* does not mean that right and wrong cease to exist. The fury of battle does not justify every act committed by a soldier, but it can certainly explain why it happened. And when we consider the adrenalin that surely flows in the midst of warfare, coupled with the existing bad blood between the Tennessee Yankees, runaway slaves, Confederate deserters, and Forrest's men, a slaughter would not be surprising.

Nevertheless, the scope of this book is not to try and explain every possible scenario of what took place at Fort Pillow. Nor is it to defend Forrest as faultless. This book's thesis would be better served if Forrest were guilty of horrendous atrocities, because it would prove in greater fashion that he was an amazingly depraved man who still found grace through Jesus Christ. I do not write as a Fort Pillow apologist, nor as a Bedford Forrest ideologue who refuses to see error where error occurs. Forrest certainly had numerous shortcomings, faults, and sins, and some of those were manifested at Fort Pillow; but to suggest that his sole purpose in attacking the fort was to massacre everyone housed there is simply inaccurate. As historian Edwin Bearss states, "If Forrest had intended a 'massacre' there would have been few, if any, survivors."[10] Couple this with the fact that Forrest had officially asked for their surrender and promised prisoner of war status to those who acquiesced, even commending the Federals for their "gallant" defense, seems to make it clear that a massacre was not Forrest's intent, at least originally. But what about after the surrender offer was rebuffed?

Undoubtedly, the makeup of the fort's inhabitants and the taunting that took place prior to the charge led to the vindictive killing of some men. Some seem to have been killed after laying down their arms and trying to surrender. While this is inexcusable, the fact that some laid down arms only to take them back up and fire again would perhaps explain why this occurred. The Confederates hated the men inside Fort Pillow, just as those inside Fort Pillow hated Forrest and his men. When mutual hatred mixes with weaponry, fueled by alcohol, mass carnage is the result, with one side eventually conquering the other. At Fort Pillow the conquerors were the Confederates, but by war's end, the conquerors would be the Federals and their atrocities were at times just as severe, if not worse. Forrest's men attacked soldiers. At times, Union commanders ordered the attack, pillage, and execution of unarmed civilians. Several of these acts were committed in Tennessee prior to Fort Pillow, with Forrest's men having knowledge of them.[11] Once again, this does not justify Fort Pillow, but it does explain the vitriol that fueled the battle.

Furthermore, the question must be asked: what role did Forrest play in the attack? As commander in charge he bore the responsibility for his men, and some testified that executions took place because Forrest had called for no quarter to be given. With this in mind, it seems clear that at the very least, Forrest may have turned a blind eye to what was sure to transpire once the fort was seized. Many times he led charges, but at Fort Pillow he stayed behind the lines for twenty minutes. While this might seem out of character for him, he had suffered an injury that could have kept him from being in the midst of the fray. Or perhaps, after being jeered by a drunken enemy, he "cut the dogs loose" for twenty minutes before calling them off.

According to both Forrest and Chalmers, once the two generals entered the fort they ordered a cease-fire and demanded no more Federals be shot. Forrest made this claim until his dying day, stating that he had actually come between his men and black Union soldiers, not allowing them to be murdered. While many would raise a skeptical eyebrow at such a suggestion, it should be noted that there were many black troops uninjured, and one wonders why all of them were not executed if a massacre was intended.

The news of Fort Pillow spread like wildfire across the North. Indeed, the preliminary facts did not bode well for Forrest's innocence. He was a former slave owner and trader, viewed by some Northerners as the epitome of Southern racism, and he was known to be a fierce fighter who killed many men in combat with his own hands—a rarity among commanding generals. Finally, it was well attested that he had a fiery temper that sometimes led him to extremes. The overwhelming conclusion was that Forrest had ordered the murders of black men and Tennessee Yankees. But a closer look at the facts leads to a different conclusion. The death rate among the Federals at Fort Pillow was somewhere between 31 and 42 percent, which is hardly a massacre by Civil War standards.[12] Furthermore, Forrest had the chance to kill others yet did not. The Federal surgeon at Fort Pillow, Charles Fitch, testified that he surrendered to one of Forrest's officers and asked to be taken to Forrest so he would be protected as a noncombatant. Fitch reported that Forrest was incensed at him for being the surgeon of a black regiment. Fitch stated that he was not, but this only drew greater ire from Forrest, who retorted that he was a "Tennessee Yankee!" Again, Fitch tried to talk his way out, only to dig his hole deeper when he stated that he was from Iowa. Forrest incredulously asked, "If you're from Iowa, then what are you doing down here?" He went on to say that Iowans had no business in Tennessee and if they had minded their own business, the war would have already been over. Forrest then ordered Fitch to be guarded and protected by his men, for which Fitch offered thanks.

There are also conflicting reports as to whether Forrest ordered black troops to be shot. When he offered the chance for surrender, he stated that the prisoner of war status would include the black troops. One Federal black troop testified that some of the Confederates were shouting to have the black soldiers shot, while other Confederates were saying they were not supposed to be shot, by orders of General Forrest. In all likelihood Forrest would not have wanted escaped slaves to be shot since being a slave owner himself, he viewed escaped slaves as property that should be returned to the owner.

So which picture of Forrest should be believed? Was he ordering executions, or was he taking prisoners and protecting them from death? Forrest biographer Jack Hurst suggests both might have been true.

His temper may have undergone one of his characteristic waxing and wanings. Angered by the taunts of black soldiers and especially by the Union refusal to surrender, necessitating

the paying of more precious Confederate lives for this victory
he had to have, he may have ragingly ordered a massacre and
even intended to carry it out—until he rode inside the fort and
viewed the horrifying result. Then, begged for his protection,
he was probably both vain enough to be flattered and sensitive
enough to respond.[13]

The next day, the Confederates flagged down a Union
riverboat and General Chalmers escorted Union captain
John G. Woodruff and other officers through the fort. They
later testified that powder burns on some of the dead Union
men indicated they were shot at close range. Chalmers
admitted that some blacks had been executed by overzealous
Confederates but that he and General Forrest had stopped
the "massacre" as soon as they entered the fort. That Forrest
put a stop to it might be viewed as an act of valor on his part,
but the fact that Chalmers used the word "massacre" did not
bode well for what had taken place.

Perhaps the entire event is summed up best by Forrest
biographer Brian Steel Willis:

> The final death toll at Fort Pillow was a heavy one for the
> Federals. There was no wholesale or premeditated massacre
> there, for had Bedford Forrest wanted to annihilate the
> garrison, he could have easily done so and would certainly have
> supervised the operation personally. Nevertheless, there was
> brutal slaughter, beyond what should have occurred. People
> died who were attempting to surrender and should have been
> spared. Although these deaths were widespread, they appear
> to have been the acts of individuals—men who were angry
> because blacks had taken up arms against them, that some of
> their neighbors had chosen to don Union uniforms, that they
> had been forced to attack a fort that should have surrendered.
> . . . For a variety of reasons, Fort Pillow became a collective
> release of pent-up anger and hatred. It became, in clinical
> terms, a group catharsis. And as the overall commander of
> the troops on the scene, some of whom carried out these acts,
> Nathan Bedford Forrest was responsible.[14]

Forrest's official report of the battle exuded the racism that was so common in his day, stating that the battle proved "negro soldiers cannot cope with Southerners" and his hope was that they would no longer be employed as combatants against them. In writing about the effects of so many wounded and dying men fleeing to the river, Forrest penned, "The river was dyed red with the blood of the enemy for 200 yards."[15] Indeed the slaughter was great.

Chapter 6

From War to Peace: 1864-1865

"He shall enter into peace: they shall rest in their beds, each one walking in his uprightness." (Isaiah 57:2 KJV)

By the spring of 1864, the tide of war was clearly turning towards Northern victory. Forrest himself recognized the Federal momentum, and though he never let on that he viewed the war as becoming unwinnable, he began to prepare for defeat. When the war commenced, he had placed forty-five of his personal slaves into service as laborers in his camp with the promise that if they worked hard he would grant them freedom at the end of the war. Years later, Forrest testified before Congress that he believed if the North won the war, slavery would be abolished and his men would go free; yet if the South won and slavery was upheld, he would still free these men because of their service. By 1864, concluding that the Confederacy would likely lose the war and fearing he might be killed, Forrest gave all the men papers granting their freedom. In spite of their newfound liberty, they continued with him for the duration of the war.

Even with Northern victory in sight, the war would drag on another year, due in large part to the persistence of soldiers like Forrest, who continued to harass the Yankee army. William Tecumseh Sherman, who had previously made the statement that "Tennessee would never be safe as long as that Devil Forrest remains," became even more obsessed with the Southern general's death or capture. After Fort Pillow, Sherman relieved Gen. Stephen A. Hurlbut of command in West Tennessee, replacing him with Cadwallader Washburn. Sherman also

assigned Samuel Sturgis, a West Point graduate, to head up the
Federal cavalry in the area, with the specific order to capture
Forrest, no matter what the cost. In preparation for this task,
Sherman had given Sturgis a force of over six thousand men,
plus artillery guns. Sherman was planning his infamous March
to the Sea, during which he promised to defeat the armies of
Joseph Johnston then move north towards Richmond, yet he
feared what Forrest might do to thwart his efforts. By severing
communication and supply lines, Forrest, even with a small
band of men, could wreak great havoc on Sherman's plans
and thus prolong the war.

On May 2, 1864, Forrest and Sturgis had their first clash
when three hundred Confederates fought with two thousand
Federals near Bolivar, Tennessee. Amazingly, Forrest's cavalry
was able to repulse the Federals with an initial charge, but the
overwhelming numbers eventually caused the Confederates
to withdraw and retreat. The Federals spent the next few
days trying to find Forrest and his men, but to no avail. Soon
Sturgis had to wire Sherman that he was unable to capture
or kill Forrest, but he tried to save face by bragging that he
had driven him out of Tennessee. A highly irritated Sherman
was unimpressed.

Brice's Crossroads

As Sherman moved on Georgia, Sturgis licked his wounds
and once again attempted to locate Forrest. In a game of
cat and mouse the two cavalries parried up and down the
Tennessee-Mississippi border. By now, Sturgis's entire force
had grown to nearly ten thousand men, while Forrest had
around forty-eight hundred. True to his form, Forrest did
not allow himself to be the pursued for very long. Though
the enemy outnumbered him two to one, he made plans for
an assault.

Several days of rain had left the roads a muddy swamp.
Forrest determined where the Yankees were, and he
determined where he wanted to pounce on them: a heavily

wooded area known as Brice's Crossroads. Knowing that the Federal cavalry would be in the lead, he decided to attack them at the crossroads where, because of the thick woods, they would not be able to tell how few men Forrest really had. Forrest believed that they would quickly send back for the infantry to reinforce them, thus bringing the infantry into his trap. He estimated it would take the infantry three hours to arrive, giving him enough time to defeat the cavalry portion of the Sturgis army. He also knew that the hot and humid weather would exhaust the infantry by the time they reached the crossroads. The perfect scenario would then be in place for Forrest and his men to dole out a whipping to the Federal force that greatly outnumbered them.

The day went down almost exactly as Forrest hoped. While the heat was draining to both sides, the outnumbered South enjoyed the element of surprise as well as the advantage of a well-planned attack. The Yankees were bewildered and had no idea how many—or how few—men they were actually facing. Forrest further helped his ruse by calling his men to show tremendous amounts of fight, thus tricking the enemy into thinking their numbers were greater than they actually were. As the muggy afternoon turned to evening, Forrest went for the Yankee jugular, moving his artillery guns into a prime position to finish off the fight. By 5:00 P.M., with dwindling amounts of ammunition, the Federals began a full and disorganized retreat.

In his official report, Samuel Sturgis would declare how doggedly his men held up under overwhelming numbers, but nothing could have been further from the truth. Sturgis had simply been outfoxed by a general who did not share his formal education but possessed an uncanny, instinctive skill at waging warfare. Though outmanned, Forrest used the land, the heat, and the element of surprise to win the day.

Sherman promptly assigned a new general, Andrew Smith, the task of tracking Forrest. Consequently, Forrest spent the summer of 1864 defending Mississippi from Yankee invasion while Sherman marched on Georgia and the Confederate leadership bickered about how to combat him. Georgia governor Joseph E. Brown, along with generals Howell Cobb and Joseph Johnston, implored Pres. Jefferson Davis to release Forrest from the defense of Mississippi and put him to work attacking Sherman's rear. They surmised that the only way to save Georgia, and ultimately the Confederacy, would be to better utilize Forrest by having him destroy Sherman's supply and communication lines. Ironically, this was the very thing that Sherman feared most, having warned his subordinates to keep Forrest busy in Mississippi to prevent it from happening.

Davis, however, chose to ignore the counsel of Brown, Cobb, and Johnston and kept Forrest in Mississippi. Perhaps the fact that Davis was a Mississippi native played a role in his decision. It should also be noted that for much of the war, Davis, a West Point graduate himself, saw Forrest as nothing more than a successful guerilla raider. Forrest's lack of education and polish unfortunately caused Davis to underestimate his abilities to organize, coordinate, lead, and motivate large groups of men. Years after the war, Davis admitted as much, saying that Forrest could and should have been better put to use by the Confederacy.

In July, Forrest suffered what was considered a tactical defeat at Tupelo, Mississippi. As Andrew Smith's army built breastworks, safely entrenching themselves, Forrest awaited Stephen D. Lee's arrival, which would bring an additional two thousand troops. On July 14, Forrest and his commanding officer, Lee, attacked the Federals, but they were unable to overtake what Forrest called an "impregnable" position. Smith burned many of the supplies in nearby Harrisburg before marching back north towards Tennessee, but the light illuminated them, and Forrest attacked. Smith's men ultimately repulsed Forrest, who was harassing their rear guard as they moved north and ultimately drew back.

Smith was credited with protecting Sherman's supply lines

from Forrest's interference, but he was also roundly criticized for not destroying Forrest. "That Devil Forrest" would remain at large and continue to cause headaches for Sherman and the Federal army.

The Memphis Raid

In August, Forrest hatched a plan to relieve pressure in northern Mississippi while at the same time moving on his adopted hometown of Memphis. Taking two thousand of his best men and placing in command two of his younger brothers who had lived with him in Memphis and thus knew the city, Forrest approached in the predawn hours of August 21, 1864. Bill Forrest was assigned the task of capturing Union general Stephen Hurlbut at his Gayoso Hotel headquarters. Bill shared many of his more famous brother's traits, including a fiery temper. In fact, he was widely thought to be more violent than Bedford. Calm when unprovoked, Bill could snap without a moment's notice and use his perfect aim to blow a hole in any would-be harasser. It was said that Bedford Forrest feared no man on earth, except for maybe his little brother Bill. Jesse Forrest was charged with capturing Gen. Cadwallader Washburn. Forrest himself planned to raid the Irving Block prison, which housed many Confederates, including some of his former men.

The raid met with only limited success. Hurlbut was out of town, so Bill's attempts to capture him proved futile. Washburn also managed to escape, albeit in his nightshirt, to nearby Fort Pickering before Jesse could nab him. Forrest's brother did, however, take Washburn's uniform as a souvenir, presenting it to Bedford later that day. Washburn's ignominious flee led Hurlbut to ridicule his commanding officer, who had replaced him because of his inability to capture Forrest. Hurlbut later snidely remarked, "They removed me from command because I couldn't keep Forrest out of West Tennessee, and now Washburn can't keep him out of his own bedroom."[1] The overwhelming Federal presence in Memphis also thwarted Forrest's plans of overtaking the Irving Block prison, and with both Hurlbut and Washburn gone, Forrest had to settle for capturing some supplies and cutting communication lines before fleeing town. However, the raid did frighten the Union army into moving some troops out of Mississippi to reinforce Memphis, which was one of Forrest's objectives.

By the fall of 1864, Forrest was completely exhausted. A workaholic by nature, he had scarcely allowed himself to leave active service for more than three years, the lone exception being a ten-day furlough he took in LaGrange, Georgia, after his falling-out with Braxton Bragg. He wrote to his commanding officer, Richard Taylor, requesting a twenty- or thirty-day furlough to regain his strength and recruit new troops. In addition to failing strength and health, Forrest wanted to tend to personal issues back in Memphis. His mother, as well as his brother John, who had been paralyzed in the Mexican War, were still living near Memphis, which was now firmly in Union hands, and Forrest feared for their safety.

Mary Ann had endured an eighteen-month period from early 1862 to late 1863 in which she had not seen Bedford or her son, William, and determined that this would not happen again. Consequently, she began staying with them, as conditions permitted, while they were encamped. Along with the wife of Capt. M. C. Gallaway, old friends from Memphis, Mary Ann would minister and care for the young boys serving under her husband, lovingly referring to them as "my soldiers." Decades after the war ended, Forrest's men would reverently remember the quiet, unassuming, godly woman who served and cared for them. For many of the boys, Bedford became a father figure, albeit at times a stern and demanding one, while Mary Ann played the role of a loving mother, praying and caring for her boys.

To the end of their days, Bedford and Mary Ann would continue to care for the soldiers who served with them, providing financial assistance out of their own pocket to help alleviate the poverty they suffered in the postwar South. Such benevolence is all the more amazing when considering that the Forrests themselves were financially strapped after the war ended. Yet, until his death, Forrest continued to attend Confederate reunions where he could fellowship with his soldiers and learn of the hardships they were facing, helping out as best he could.

In early December 1864, during a fight near Murfreesboro, Forrest rode to each infantry regiment and took the flag from the colorbearer, trying to rally the men who were in retreat. As he came upon the colorbearer for the Fifty-Fourth Virginia Infantry, a small, smooth-faced boy named Richard Alley, Forrest barked for the flag but was surprisingly rejected: "General Forrest, I can take care of my own flag." An impressed General Forrest explained that he wanted to rally the troops, but Alley would not budge. "General, just show me where to plant it!" The boy held his ground, rallied the men, and forever won the admiration of his general. Afterwards, anytime Forrest would see the boy around camp he would salute him, and Alley would droop his flag to the general. Forrest would proudly smile and say, "There goes that little feller that totes his own flag."[2]

For the remainder of the war, Forrest would lead raids in Tennessee, Mississippi, and Alabama, eventually coming under the command of John Bell Hood, who would serve as the last general over the Army of Tennessee. In December 1864, Hood's forces were devastated in the ill-fated Battle of Nashville. As Hood retreated with what was left of his army, Forrest's cavalry guarded the rear and sufficiently protected the army so they could escape. For this, Forrest was granted his final promotion of the war to lieutenant general, thus making him the only man on either side to go from private to lieutenant general during the course of the war.

By the beginning of 1865, the Confederacy was clearly losing, and every battle was seen as a last-ditch attempt to save the South. Forrest, his cavalry, and the Army of Tennessee

Forrest later in the war with graying hair and increased signs of fatigue. (United States Library of Congress)

fought valiantly, but ultimately it would prove to be a lost cause. For Forrest, the end would come in the spring of 1865 at Selma, Alabama. Surrounded by Federals, Forrest quickly built fortifications around the city and used local militia and private citizens to supplement his troops in defense of the town. But the Federal numbers were simply too great. With dwindling ammunition and crippling exhaustion, Forrest told his men to "cut their way out" by whatever means they could. Forrest charged directly at one section of the Federal army and managed to escape only after engaging in fierce hand-to-hand combat with several Union troops, including a captain who repeatedly slashed at Forrest with his saber. Though his arm was cut and bloodied, he was able to pull his pistol and kill the captain in what would be his final casualty of the war.

During these last days of the war, a reflective Forrest began to contemplate his past and his future. He penned a heartfelt letter to his son, William, in which he encouraged him to shun his father's "wicked and sinful ways." Sounding like a man who was beginning to regret his past sins and like a father who may not live to see his son grow older, Forrest spoke proudly of what William was becoming. Bedford had kept William close throughout the war as an aide on his staff, and he had purposely assigned other young men of virtuous character to the staff to serve as friends for his son. Bedford exhorted William to take care of his mother, Mary Ann, and if he was tempted to choose between her "Christian ways" and his father's "wicked ways," to emulate her. Bedford wrote:

> If I have been wicked and sinful myself, it would rejoice my heart to see you leading the Christian life which has adorned your mother. . . . What I desire most of you my son is never to gamble or swear. These are baneful vices. As I grow older I see the folly of these two vices, and beg that you will never engage in them. . . . Be honest, be truthful, in all your dealings with the world. Be cautious in the selection of your friends. Shun the society of

the low and vulgar. Strive to elevate your character and to take a high and honorable position in society. . . . Keep this letter prominently before you . . . should we meet no more on earth.[3]

Clearly, at this point, Forrest was entertaining thoughts of his possible death or was perhaps contemplating a flight to Mexico. It is also fairly obvious that spiritual matters were beginning to take on new importance in his life. The war was nearing an end, and his son had become a man. Forrest had been saved from death time and time again, and deep down he knew there was a reason for it. He was no novice where matters of Christianity were concerned. His mother and wife were both extremely devout, and he had sat under the preaching of countless army chaplains over the last four years, including D. C. Kelley, the Methodist minister who served as one of his top subordinates. Forrest was indeed thinking about his future and musing about his past. And he did not like what he saw. Forrest had many positive virtues, but he had led a life of sin, and he knew it. So well did he know it that he encouraged his son to avoid following in his footsteps.

Nathan Bedford Forrest had devoted four years of his life to a war he was about to lose, and such a major event caused him to be unusually reflective. During this time of intense soul searching, he came face-to-face with his sinful past and feared the effect it might have on his only son. Jesus told Nicodemus that he "must be born again" (John 3:3 NASB). He must experience a spiritual birth just as he experienced a physical birth. A genuine, God-inspired change needed to touch his heart. The same was true for Forrest. He would have to feel conviction and contrition over his sin and repentantly place his faith in Jesus as Lord in order to find redemption. This is what the Bible calls all sinners to do. This would be what Nathan Bedford Forrest would have to do.

Undoubtedly the Spirit of God had been convicting Forrest for many years, but it was a conviction he fought tooth and nail. He knew he should do things differently, but he always said he did not have time for serious religion while there was so much "unholy fighting" to be done. It never seemed to dawn on him that men like Kelley, as well as scores of other Christian soldiers, saw service in battle to one's country and service in life to one's Lord as compatible. Men like the pious Stonewall Jackson proved that one could be a devout Christian and fierce warrior at the same time. But Forrest could not seem to reconcile the two in his mind. Perhaps he did not want to.

Forrest could see clearly how the hand of God had protected him throughout the war. One has to wonder what was going through his mind as he saw thousands and thousands of men fall in death while he repeatedly escaped. Many times throughout the course of the war he was in situations where he could have and probably should have died. The bullets would either barely miss him or they would strike yet land millimeters away from vital organs in his body. So many near-death experiences had to have had a spiritual effect upon him. He later attributed his survival in battle to the prayers of his wife and mother, so he knew there was a spiritual aspect to it, but his pride would not allow him to submit his entire life and being to Jesus Christ as Lord. Forrest had to be in control at all times, and submitting to Christ as Lord meant relinquishing control. And this he would not do. He respected religion; he revered Christians and had a close relationship with many ministers who served the Southern army; he was proud that his wife was a believer and clearly reaped the benefits of Mary Ann's piety; he wanted his son to be a Christian man who would live a life devoted to the Lord, rather than a life of sin, but Forrest could not submit to Christ. At least he would not yet.

The war was drawing to a close and many wondered aloud what Forrest, and others like him, would do. Several Confederates contemplated a flight to Mexico where they could escape any possible charges of treason. Others, including Pres. Jefferson Davis, advocated a guerilla-type war to be waged against the "Yankee invaders" until such time as they won victory. Indeed, guerilla-type tactics had been used admirably by men such as Francis Marion in the American Revolution, and skilled and stealth cavalrymen like Forrest would no doubt be able to harass the Federals indefinitely. Gen. Robert E. Lee was faced with this option prior to his surrender at Appomattox, but he refused to take it. He surmised that a guerilla army would lack discipline and order and would most certainly become nothing more than a roving group of bandits, and he wanted no part of it. Lee believed such a war could go on for twenty years and turn America into an indeterminate bloodbath. In his mind, the war had been courageously waged, but to no avail. As Lee surrendered to Ulysses S. Grant, and Joseph Johnston surrendered to William Sherman, Forrest considered his options. He took his remaining men and camped near Gainesville, Alabama, to sort things out.

On two successive nights, Forrest went for rides in the country with Maj. Charles Anderson, whose eloquent hand had penned so many of his orders. While the soldiers back in camp were weary from the war, some of the younger ones sought to fight on by way of taking to the hills in guerilla fashion or going to Mexico. Forrest seriously considered both options. At one point on their ride, Forrest and Anderson came to a fork in the road. After pausing for a few moments, Anderson asked, "Which way General?" Forrest responded, "Either. If one road led to hell and the other to Mexico, I would be indifferent as to which to take."[4]

On this fateful night, Major Anderson earned his keep. He helped Forrest sort out the issues and reminded him that many young men back at camp would be looking to him for guidance. Mexican exile or guerilla warfare might sound glamorous to the young, but someone of Forrest's maturity knew that it was no way to live. Much as Lee painfully made the decision to surrender to Grant, famously saying, "There's nothing left to do but go see Grant, and I would rather die a thousand deaths," Forrest also made up his mind, although in fewer words. After hearing Anderson's recommendation that he surrender, Forrest softly answered with three: "That settles it."

The second night Forrest and Anderson rode out of camp to work on his final speech to his troops. Forrest would lay down his arms and call his men to do the same—but not before one more attempt was made to get him to fight guerilla style. Mississippi governor Charles Clark and former Tennessee governor Isham Harris convened with Forrest, encouraging him to fight on. Forrest responded, "You men can do as you damn well please, I'm a-goin' home. Any man who is in favor of a further prosecution of this war is a fit subject for a lunatic asylum, and should be sent there immediately."[5]

While Forrest was a fierce fighter who was willing to repeatedly risk his life against overwhelming odds, he was also a realist and he knew the time had come to end hostilities. In his farewell address to his men he said,

> Reason dictates and humanity demands that no more blood be shed . . . it is your duty and mine to lay down our arms— submit to the powers that be and to aid in restoring peace and establishing law and order throughout the land. . . . Civil war, such as you have just passed through, naturally engenders feelings of animosity, hatred, and revenge. It is our duty to divest ourselves of all such feelings; and as far as is in our power to do so, to cultivate friendly feelings toward those with whom we have so long contended and heretofore so widely, but honestly differed. Neighborhood feuds, personal animosities, and private differences should be blotted out; and when you return home, a manly, straight forward course of conduct will secure the respect even of your enemies. Whatever your responsibility may be to government, to society, or to individuals meet them like men. . . . I have never, on the field of battle, sent you where I was unwilling to go myself; nor would I now advise you to a course which I felt myself unwilling to pursue. You have been good soldiers; you can be good citizens. Obey the laws, preserve your honor, and the government

to which you have surrendered can afford to be, and will be magnanimous.[6]

Finally, after four long, hard-fought years of battle, countless nights sleeping in the elements, numerous hand-to-hand confrontations, twenty-nine dead horses, four bullet wounds, and scores of bumps, cuts, scrapes, and bruises, Nathan Bedford Forrest, was "a-goin' home."

Chapter 7

The Trials of Reconstruction

"To every thing there is a season, and a time to every purpose under the heaven: a time to be born, and a time to die; a time to plant, and a time to pluck up that which is planted; a time to kill, and a time to heal; a time to break down, and a time to build up." (Ecclesiastes 3:1-3 KJV)

While the war raged, none were more committed to the cause than Nathan Bedford Forrest. But once the war ended, Forrest made every effort to put the past four years behind him and begin the task of readjusting to a peacetime existence. For most Southerners, Confederate patriotism ran deep. Years after the war, Confederate stalwarts would mourn the "lost cause" and analyze, blame, and reminisce about the reasons why they lost the war and what might have been had they won. Animosity continued between North and South in many circles, with anger growing deeper as a result of Northern Reconstruction, which sought to punish the South for their "rebellion" towards their Federal masters. While Forrest was leery and untrusting of the Northern carpetbaggers whom he felt sought to exploit a ravaged South for personal gain, Forrest also considered the war to be a noble effort that was lost and now should be placed in the past. Always a man of shrewd financial acumen, Forrest began the work of rebuilding business in a postwar, post-slavery society. And in so doing, he was more than willing to work with Southern as well as Northern brethren in order to reestablish his name and once again work towards financial security.

The war had changed his life's circumstances dramatically, in more ways than one. Financially, he had a lot of work to do. Forrest had claimed that before the war began he had a personal fortune of $1.5 million, which would be an astronomical sum in nineteenth-century currency. His slave trading and plantations had been extremely successful, and by anyone's account he would have been a very wealthy man. Yet, during the war, amidst the financial struggles of the fledgling Confederacy, Forrest frequently supplied arms and equipment to his men out of his own pocket. He seemed to understand that if the Confederacy lost the war, he would lose his fortune anyway, so he gave all he had to the cause. Slave trading was no longer an option, but he had already abandoned that before the war. Farming would be his initial means for making money, and at war's end, he promptly planted his first crop of postwar corn. In addition to his farming, Forrest opened a sawmill in Coahoma County, Mississippi, in order to supply lumber to an area that would need to be rebuilt after four years of ravaging war. Not only would this provide additional income for him, but it would also supply several jobs for those who sorely needed them. Then he set about renting out some of his plantation land to other veterans, both Northern and Southern. Seven Federal officers rented land from him, and he helped them cultivate it for agricultural use.

While Forrest was kind towards his former enemies, he was also working a bit of an angle as he sought to reestablish his finances. Having former Union officers as friends and business partners would help him land free blacks to work his farm as well as grant him a certain amount of credibility in the Federal government's eyes. He had promptly applied for a pardon from Pres. Andrew Johnson but would have to wait three years for it to be granted. Having taken the loyalty oath, he sought to become once more a "Union man" and encouraged his former soldiers to exhibit faithfulness to the government to which they once again belonged. Far from being angry at his losses after the war, Forrest worked as hard as anyone in Western Tennessee to bond the fractured parties back together or in Lincoln's words, "bind up the nation's wounds."

One of the Federals who would provide a sterling character witness for Forrest was Gen. Frank Blair. Having fought fiercely to keep Missouri in Union hands, Blair went on to become a major general serving under William Tecumseh Sherman, the man who christened Forrest "that Devil." After the war, Blair met Forrest in Memphis, but he was highly skeptical of his former enemy, for good reason. Forrest had made Blair's life miserable for the duration of the war, and there was no one Sherman had wanted stopped more than Forrest. Add to this Forrest's reputation as the "butcher of Fort Pillow" and it is easy to see why Blair would approach Forrest coolly. Yet, he found Forrest to be nothing like he expected. Blair endorsed Forrest's application for parole and sent it to his brother, Montgomery Blair, who had served as Lincoln's postmaster general. He in turn presented it to President Johnson. Frank Blair wrote of Forrest: "I have conceived a very great personal attachment for Forrest. . . . His noble bearing since the war in accepting without complaint the result and using his powerful influence to make others accept it in the same spirit, have inspired me with a respect and admiration I have not felt for any other man."[1]

But Blair's words did not have the desired effect. Though Forrest was beloved in the South, he was still scorned in the North. Fueled by an extremely influential media that despised him, Northerners read frequent editorials in newspapers calling for the execution of Confederate leaders for treason, with some of the loudest jeers being reserved for Forrest. Most of these newspaper men had never met Forrest and like Blair, they were basing their opinions of his peacetime attitude on wartime exploits, unsubstantiated rumors, and even downright lies. Nevertheless, Forrest had his faults, and one Northern writer who actually interviewed him described Forrest as a rare individual who while being a "braggart" was actually willing and able to back up his boasts with action. His pride and his prowess were both apparent to those who knew him. But so was his sense of justice and this would be tested early in 1866.

Thomas Edwards was a black employee on Forrest's plantation and according to accounts by blacks and whites alike, he was an insolent and hot-tempered man. Like the other workers on the plantation he lived with his wife in a cabin provided by Forrest, but unlike the others, Edwards had a well-known reputation for beating his wife. The trouble began when Edwards confronted his foreman, B. F. Diffenbocker, a former Union major, over a pay dispute. In the midst of this argument, other issues also arose, and Diffenbocker confronted Edwards over the treatment of his wife, reminding him that "wife beating was against General Forrest's rules of conduct." For all Forrest's faults, he seems to have retained a lifelong respect for women and bristled at the sight of them being mistreated. Cruelty towards women simply would not be tolerated according to Forrest's Southern code of honor. He also had a deep love for animals and frequently during the war rebuked soldiers who were unnecessarily harsh towards their horses. Like many Southern country boys, he grew up with a love for dogs and horses and hated to see any animal mistreated. When word reached him that Edwards, a well-known wife beater, had also beaten a mule to death, Forrest was livid.

The Edwards-Diffenbocker exchange ended with Edwards reportedly proclaiming, "I will whip my wife whenever I please. I do not care for General Forrest or any other man. If General Forrest or any other man attempts to interfere with me, I'll cut his guts out." If Edwards did indeed say this, as Diffenbocker testified, it was a grave mistake. A man who had already been marked by Forrest as an enemy was now on even shakier ground due to his insulting attitude towards his boss. Tensions ran high, and they exploded on March 31.

Some stagnant pools of water had accumulated near the workers' cabins, and Forrest, fearing cholera, came to inspect them and have them drained. He called on Edwards and some of the other workers to help dig a drainage ditch, but Edwards refused, yelling loudly at Forrest that he was going to his cabin to eat his dinner—and if his dinner was not ready he would make his wife pay. A few moments later, the familiar pained screams of Mrs. Edwards began to emanate from the cabin, along with the sound of Mr. Edwards' whip. This was something that had happened numerous times before, occasionally even requiring a doctor's care. Forrest heard all he cared to hear and true to his nature, promptly acted.

Entering the cabin, Forrest told Edwards to stop abusing his wife, to which Edwards responded that he would beat her anytime he pleased, then continued cursing Forrest. According to Forrest's account, he then warned Edwards that he would not be talked to that way, and if he did not cease, then he would deal with him physically. Edwards continued, and Forrest picked up a broom handle and smacked him on the head. Edwards then pulled a knife and lunged at Forrest, cutting his hand. The brawl continued for a few moments, until both men made a move towards an axe that was lying in the corner. Forrest got there first and ended the fight, and Edwards' life, with a swift blow to the head. Thomas Edwards was dead. Nathan Bedford Forrest had killed him. Was it justifiable homicide? Forrest was content to allow the courts to decide. He sent for the law and then returned to his house to await their arrival.

Of the two hundred freemen working the plantation, it appears that most were content with Forrest as an employer. After the incident he offered all of them release from their contract, but only eighteen chose this route. Nevertheless, there appears to have been a group of disgruntled workers who saw Edwards as their ringleader. Several of these freemen gathered around Forrest's home with bonfires lit. Accounts vary as to what took place during this time. Some say that Forrest at one point went out on the porch and calmly gave his side of the story, telling the men that the law would soon sort it out. Another account says that Forrest waved pistols from the porch and promised to shoot anyone who threatened him. Whatever the case, around midnight a deputy named

Wirt Shaw arrived and cautiously made his way to the front of the house, knocked, identified himself, and explained why he was there. Forrest called through the door, "It's alright. You've got me. Come in." The two men agreed that it would be safer to wait until morning to depart, giving the crowd time to disperse, which they did without incident.

Forrest was charged with killing Edwards and was released on ten thousand dollars' bail pending his trial, which was set for October. While testimony was conflicting, the majority of it favored Forrest's account. The two eyewitnesses were Thomas Edwards's wife and a girl named Hannah Powell, who lived with the Edwardses. Mrs. Edwards defended her husband, which is fairly common among abused wives, who are accustomed to living in fear and in denial of their husband's actions. Powell sided with Forrest's account, though she said her view was blocked by Forrest and she could not see if Edwards pulled a knife or not.

Ironically, one of the witnesses siding with Forrest was Capt. N. D. Collins of the local Freedman's Bureau. The Bureau had been set up to deal with any complaints former slaves had regarding discrimination by white employers or citizens. Having investigated Forrest's plantation, Captain Collins concluded that Forrest did indeed have some faults towards the black freemen working his land. Collins stated that Forrest was far too lenient and benevolent towards them because he paid wages much higher than most plantations did, and he allowed the black workers to buy and possess firearms. Some would suggest that this was simply Forrest's way of trying to prove to the government how gracious he was towards the freemen and thus perhaps gain his much-coveted pardon, but clearly it shows that oppression, aggression, and persecution were not marks of his demeanor towards his black employees. Collins "did not think the ex-slaves could handle the type of freedom and personal responsibility that Forrest was granting them and recommended that he no longer tolerate armed employees on his land," referring to Forrest as "too liberal a character."[2] Today, it is almost humorous to imagine that many oppose Forrest for his racist views while he was described as being too liberal regarding black civil rights in his own day.

Forrest was exonerated of the charges, with the jury finding that while he may have struck the first blow with a broom handle, he had adequate reason to suspect Edwards intended bodily harm towards him, and thus his actions were considered self-defense.

While Forrest's legal troubles were now over, his financial problems increased. A combination of legal fees and poor crop production left him greatly in debt, and he was forced to sell much of his land. Parole restrictions from the war hindered his travel, so he once again petitioned President Johnson's help. In a gracious letter to the president, he admitted that he was seen by many in the North as a monster, but that he in fact had a strong desire for peace. While saying that he felt he deserved full amnesty, he understood Johnson's reluctance to grant it due to the political fallout it would cause. He did, however, request the ability to travel more broadly for business purposes. Johnson granted formal permission and kept Forrest's letter to show others a "model example of what the true restorationist of the South should have been."[3]

It was about this time that Tennessee firebrand and loyal Unionist William Brownlow ascended to the governorship of the state, and tensions reached cataclysmic heights. Brownlow was a former Methodist minister and newspaper editor of the *Knoxville Whig* who prior to the war was a slave owner yet remained an ardent and fiery Unionist. His rhetoric aimed at secessionists made him a loathsome figure to many in the South, and in 1862 he was arrested and jailed by the Confederacy. He petitioned Jefferson Davis for release, promising to leave Tennessee and relocate north if granted freedom. Davis granted it, and Brownlow left. While in the North he continued to make a name for himself by delivering scorching speeches aimed at his fellow Tennesseans and

Southerners. In 1863, after East Tennessee was again under Union control, Brownlow returned and renewed his writing campaign against the Confederacy. His time in prison had only further emboldened him, and when elected governor in 1865, shortly after the war, he had vengeance on his mind.

The election of 1865 was unique in that many Tennesseans who had served the Confederacy were banned from voting. While the free blacks did not vote in 1865, a policy that Brownlow agreed with, they were granted voting rights in 1867 and gave Brownlow a thorough reelection. Under his reign, martial law was established in Tennessee, and Confederate punishment was a common theme of the governor's administration. He spoke of seizing Confederate veterans' land and giving it to pro-Union citizens. He spoke of arresting or even lynching former Confederates. And in so doing, he managed to fan flames of resentment that already burned hot. In one postwar speech, Brownlow exclaimed:

> I am one of those who believe the war has ended too soon. We have whipped the rebels, but not enough. The loyal masses constitute an overwhelming majority of the people of this country, and they intend to march again on the South, and intend this second war shall be no child's play. The second army of invasion will, as they ought to, make the entire South as God found the earth, without form and void. They will not, and ought not to, leave one rebel fence-rail, outhouse, one dwelling, in the eleven seceded States. As for the Rebel population, let them be exterminated. When the second war is wound up, which should be done with swift destruction, let the land be surveyed and sold out to pay expenses.[4]

In another postwar speech, he suggested a new three-phase armed invasion of the South with the first army given the task of killing, the second army given the task of burning, and the third army assigned to surveying the land and redistributing it to loyal Unionists.[5] Not surprisingly, his talk of renewed hostilities, mass murder of Confederate soldiers and private citizens, and Federal seizure of land made him despised by many of his constituents.

In the midst of this political and racial powder keg, a small group of men from Pulaski, Tennessee, banned together and started to multiply. This secret organization claimed they existed to protect white people from radical Reconstructionists and militant freemen. The group would rapidly grow and become deeply enmeshed in the turmoil of the times, continuing to live in infamy today. Even Forrest would play a role in this group's rise to prominence. Named for the Greek word *kyklos,* for "circle," they would come to be known as the Ku Klux Klan.

Chapter 8

The Klan and the Railroads

"All my ways are before You." (Psalms 119:168 NASB)

One of the most common myths surrounding Nathan Bedford Forrest is that he was the founder of the Ku Klux Klan. Nothing could be further from the truth. However, once a myth is propagated over a long period of time, it becomes truth in most eyes, regardless of the facts that prove otherwise. The Forrest-as-Klan-founder myth has been accepted for so long that it has even seeped into popular culture, as evidenced by its continuation, for example, in the 1990s epic *Forrest Gump.* In the movie, the backwards Southerner Gump is supposedly named after his ancestor Nathan Bedford Forrest who, as Gump tells the story, used to ride around in white sheets and scare people. In fact, even a perusal of the name "Forrest" in many encyclopedias and dictionaries will reference the name as "an American Confederate general who was the founder and first leader of the Ku Klux Klan"[1] Forrest's founding of the Ku Klux Klan is a fascinating story. The problem is that it is not true. But his involvement in the Klan is.

The Klan's origins can be traced to Pulaski, Tennessee, where a small group of six Confederate veterans sat around a fire and reminisced about the war. The men were John C. Lester, John B. Kennedy, James R. Crowe, Frank O. McCord, Richard Reed, and J. Calvin Jones. As they talked they decided to form a secret society that would ride in costume to intimidate Northern carpetbaggers and black people. The atmosphere among Southern whites during this time was one of great fear and paranoia, albeit for legitimate reasons.

The freedmen and the carpetbagging Yankees who came south to make money both seemed to have the full support of Governor Brownlow to do what they wished with the secessionists. This fear led to night patrols being organized in many white communities, where men would guard the town and surrounding areas against any potential harm. Within a short amount of time the night patrols and the intimidating nocturnal activities of the Klan began to merge.

Also, rather quickly, the Klan began to grow in number, and men across Tennessee and eventually the entire South joined. However, the organization had no real structure, no clear leadership, and no set agenda or mission. At one extreme were agitated, angry young men who sought to terrorize all who opposed them. These thought nothing of lynching and intimidation and were, for all practical purposes, thugs who sought to expand power by inciting fear. At the other extreme were professional "pillars of society" who joined to show solidarity against the radical Reconstruction policies of the Brownlow administration and who honestly feared for the safety of their families and friends. Such men truly saw the Klan as a protective, paramilitary organization that would help keep the peace in a Southern world gone mad. The dilemma early on was over who would gain control and what would the organizational objectives be.

By the spring of 1867, two former Confederate generals had stepped into the leadership vacuum of the Klan and assumed administrative oversight for the sprouting organization. Neither of these generals was Forrest. Both Pulaski natives, George Gordon and John C. Brown took the reins and planned a major meeting for Nashville later in the spring.

Another one of the early Klan leaders was John Morton, the former chief of Forrest's artillery, who appears to be the one who initiated Forrest into the group. Morton claims that Forrest approached him about joining and that Morton put him off for a while before eventually telling his old general to raise his right hand and repeat the oath.

The original Ku Klux Klan was clearly a racist organization that opposed black equality, yet some of its earlier aims were a far cry from what the group would eventually degenerate into. Their mission statement claimed they were "an instrument of Chivalry, Humanity, Mercy, and patriotism" who saw it as one of their primary motives to "relieve and assist the injured, oppressed, suffering, and unfortunate, especially widows and orphans of Confederate soldiers; and to support the United States Constitution and Constitutional Laws."[2]

Their fears were not limited to physical safety, as many in the organization harbored nightmare scenarios of newly freed slaves sitting in political offices, acting as puppets for the white Yankees who had come south to make a fortune under government-funded "reconstruction." The economic future of the South was at stake, and whatever means necessary were to be employed to keep further disaster from coming. This is one reason why some Klansmen sought to deter blacks from going to the voting booths during postwar elections.

Others naively thought the former slaves would be faithful to their former masters and vote for conservative Democrats, but in the elections of 1867 this did not happen. With newly freed slaves voting Republican, and many former Confederates banned from voting, the radicals won the day, and the already toxic atmosphere was further poisoned. At this point the Klan went from a group focused on scaring black people away from the voting booths to a group that would employ physical methods to accomplish their aims. They foolishly thought the blacks would vote Democratic, and in their humiliation they vowed to make sure that black people, influenced by Yankees, would not further damage the South.

In February 1868, after a white man was robbed and killed by a black man, Klansmen entered the jail, kidnapped the prisoner, and lynched him. Other beatings and acts of intimidation took place across Tennessee and beyond as the Klan tried to spread greater fear. But what was Forrest's role in this escalation of hostilities?

Forrest claimed to have always been opposed to acts of violence against blacks. While undoubtedly he was aware of and probably advocated some of the intimidation tactics, he did not seem to believe that violence would solve any problems. The war had left him beat up, exhausted, and weary of the fight. And while he still had that same fiery temper and fighter's instincts, he seems to have genuinely sought peace apart from the sword . . . or the noose.

From the Nashville meeting of spring 1867 onward, Forrest appears to have held the leadership role of grand wizard. Many within the group sought an experienced veteran with widespread name recognition to lead the growing organization, and Forrest, who was a bigger name than any other Tennessee veteran, seemed the obvious choice. His job would be to oversee the group and receive reports from subordinate commanders throughout the South. He would also actively recruit for the Klan as their administrative figurehead. In the latter role, his newfound work in insurance would play an active part.

Forrest would accept the position as president of the Planters Life Insurance Company in May 1867 after seeing his plantations and sawmill flounder. In his insurance role, he traveled across the South seeking to drum up business and meet with other insurance contacts. In so doing, he more than likely also recruited for the Klan while conferring with other high-ranking Klan officials. By March 1868, Planters had gone bankrupt and Forrest was required to once again find new work.

During this same time, Forrest became a partner in a paving company, with plans to sell "paving bonds" as a means to improve Memphis streets. Within a short amount of time, this venture also failed due to a lack of worthy investors. With the economy on such shaky ground, few were willing to invest in these bonds, which brought little if any return.

A brief stint with the Southern Life Insurance Company as an agent granted Forrest an income, and perhaps cover for Klan activities. But this position was also short lived.

As an example of how perilous the times were, Forrest considered raising a group of former Confederates to invade Mexico. Having become so disenfranchised with American Reconstruction, Forrest was of the opinion that he could recruit thousands of volunteers and overtake Mexico rather easily. With a new nation conquered, he would be able to renew the Confederate dreams south of the American border.

How seriously he really considered this plan is hard to say. The days were so desperate that any and all possibilities for the future were considered, but this pipe dream fizzled rather quickly. Maybe he was just bored. Maybe he missed the excitement of combat and conquest more than he thought. Maybe he feared for his future in America. Whatever motivated him seems to have subsided while the scheme was still in the planning stages.

As the nation approached the elections of 1868, Forrest took a more active role in the political process. He wrote a letter to the editor of the *Memphis Avalanche* in which he expressed fear that unless conservative Tennesseans stood up, the state would be destroyed by radical Reconstructionists. He was then appointed as a representative to the Tennessee Democratic Convention. Forrest had no personal political ambitions and was banned from holding office because of his high-ranking status in the Confederate army. Nevertheless, he sought to have his voice heard and wanted to assist in the peace process that heretofore had failed in Tennessee.

At the state convention in Nashville, some controversy swirled due to a block of delegates desiring Forrest's nomination as a delegate to the upcoming Democratic National Convention. While some saw him as an unnecessary lightning rod for the party, others considered him to be the very type of person they needed as a delegate. A mixture of pro-Union and former Confederates seemed to give adequate representation to all parties involved, but Forrest's presence as a delegate would surely provide greater influence for the conservative branch. Though he did not actively seek the nomination, he would

A picture of Forrest in uniform, later in life. (Courtesy of Tennessee State Library & Archives)

not refuse it either. Claiming that he wanted to be of service however they saw fit to use him, he was eventually nominated after much debate. Nathan Bedford Forrest would be going to New York for the Democratic National Convention as a delegate from Tennessee, and trouble was almost certain to follow.

As the train chugged northward toward New York, Forrest sat relaxing in his seat. A scheduled stop lay just ahead, where the train would break and the passengers could exit for a short respite. But the schedule and the controversial passenger were both known to the townspeople, and a mob assembled at the train station to meet Forrest. The mob's ringleader was a massive, hot-tempered man well-known for his fighting prowess who swore he would "thrash that butcher Forrest." Seeking to avoid a fight, the train conductor approached Basil Duke, former Confederate general and delegate from Kentucky, asking him to request that Forrest stay in his seat to avoid trouble. Duke approached Forrest, who willingly and calmly submitted, having stated that people seeking his life was not that uncommon and he saw no reason to be excited about it. The mob's ringleader did not share Forrest's pacifism and barged onto the train.

In this instance, we have a clear example of an occasion where Forrest did not seek trouble, yet trouble still found him. All his life he had struggled with a violent temper when provoked. In fact he had the reputation in battle of transforming into another person when challenged. The switch would flip and Forrest would come unglued, eager to defend himself. This is exactly what happened on the train. As Duke recounted: "I never in my life witnessed such an instantaneous and marvelous transformation in any one's appearance. Erect and dilated, his face the color of heated bronze, and his eyes flaming, blazing. He strode rapidly down the aisle toward the approaching champion, his gait and manner evincing perfect, invincible determination."[3] The man bellowed, "Where's that butcher Forrest." And quickly, "that butcher Forrest" was right in his face. "I'm Forrest! What do you want?" the general replied. At this point the would-be assailant had a quick change of heart. The combination of Forrest's courage, fiery appearance, and willingness to fight apparently shocked the man, who turned and scurried from the train, running past the crowd, losing his hat in his flight. Forrest gave chase, calling him to come back, until he reached the platform, where he stopped and laughed. The mob, by this point settled after witnessing their leader flee, nervously laughed along with Forrest for a few minutes before he returned to his seat with the situation diffused.

Upon arriving at the convention, Forrest played a very low-key role, at least publicly. He gave no speeches and made no nominations. Behind the scenes he tried to secure votes for the Tennessee native, Andrew Johnson, who had recently escaped impeachment by a very small margin. But Johnson was not to win the day, the nomination going to New York's Horatio Seymour on the twenty-third ballot. Seymour would go on to lose the general election to the Republican war hero, Ulysses S. Grant, who would serve two terms during the controversial Reconstruction years.

Forrest's reputation continued to dog him, even in New York, where many newspapers wrote derisive editorials about his presence. One morning, a lady knocked at his hotel door before he was out of bed. His son, William, answered the door to see the agitated woman burst into the room, walk up to Bedford, and ask if the story that he had killed the innocent people at Fort Pillow was true. Forrest, disheveled and sleepy-eyed, stood up and barked, "Yes, madam. I killed the men and women for my soldiers' dinner and ate the babies myself for breakfast."[4] The woman ran screaming from the room, and Forrest enjoyed a snicker. The sarcastic response showed that he was getting tired of answering for Fort Pillow.

After the convention, Forrest returned home to Tennessee and found that the schism between the Klan and the government had widened. Governor Brownlow had spoken of calling out a state militia to oppose the Klan, deeming them an outlaw organization. Indeed, some branches were as the problems of control and purpose continued to afflict the organization. While some leaders, including Forrest, publicly condemned all violence by the Klan, others carried out acts of intimidation, either of their own accord or under orders from a higher power. To his grave, Forrest would claim that he opposed violent means of persuasion and that he did everything within his ability to see the perpetrators brought to justice. Regardless of what he said, many would never believe the former slave trader and "butcher of Fort Pillow."

If in fact Forrest and other Klan leaders saw the group as a defensive and protective organization meant to protect Southern whites, especially the widows and orphans of Confederate soldiers, then it would be easy to see why they would be so fiercely enraged when Brownlow called them outlaws. If some of the Klan leaders were seeking to bring peace for all races by opposing radical Reconstructionism, then it is understandable that they would be incensed at being accused of spreading violence. On the other hand, some supposed Klan members were guilty of violent acts. Clearly the situation in Tennessee after the war was confusing and volatile, with claims and counterclaims being made by both sides. For a time there seemed to be a genuine threat of a reignited Civil War, a war that most did not want but some would be willing to fight again.

Ironically, according to Forrest, his problems were not with the black freedmen so much as they were with the white Northerners, whom he felt were stirring up trouble in the South. In a speech given at Brownsville, Tennessee, Forrest railed against the governor, stating that he believed Brownlow lumped all former Confederates together as Klansmen and that the governor was seeking to pass laws that would allow citizens to shoot them on sight without fear of prosecution. If these laws were passed, Forrest said that another war would commence, though he himself had no desire to see that happen. He ended the speech by saying, "If they bring this war upon us, there is one thing I will tell you—that I shall not shoot any negroes so long as I can see a white Radical to shoot, for it is the Radicals who will be to blame for bringing on this war."[5]

While 1869 saw the inauguration of Ulysses S. Grant as president, it also brought an unexpected and pleasant surprise for Forrest and the Tennessee Democrats. Governor Brownlow, public enemy number one and longtime nemesis, resigned as governor to become a United States senator from Tennessee. His replacement, DeWitt Senter, sought to work with Democrats in the state and made efforts to appease men like Forrest. With Brownlow gone, Forrest saw no further need for the Ku Klux Klan and ordered them disbanded. General Order Number One from Klan headquarters, dated January 25, 1869, presumably written by Forrest, states:

> Whereas, The Order of the K.K.K. is in some localities being perverted from its original honorable and patriotic purposes; And whereas, such a perversion of the Order is in some instances defeating the very objects of its origin, and is becoming injurious instead of subservient to the public peace and public safety for which it was intended, and in some cases is being used to achieve personal benefit and private purposes, and to satiate private revenge by means of its masked features. It is therefore ordered and decreed, that the masks and costumes of this Order be entirely abolished and destroyed. And every Grand Cyclops shall assemble the men of his Den and require them to destroy in his presence every article of his mask and costume and at the same time shall destroy his own. And every man who shall refuse to do so shall be deemed an enemy of this Order and shall be treated accordingly. And every man who shall hereafter be seen in mask or costume, shall not be known or recognized as a member of this Order, but shall be deemed an enemy of the same.[6]

While most historians attribute the order to Forrest as grand wizard, Forrest himself always maintained that he was never an actual member but merely a supporter and adviser to the group. Even in the advisory role he claimed, he recommended the organization's disbandment by 1869. Always a man who craved control and order, he no doubt saw that the Klan was now uncontrollable, with various sects and groups perpetrating violence without the consent of headquarters or his own approval. He sought to distance himself from the Klan and in time would boldly speak out and even threaten them for their violent ways.

In 1871, Forrest would be called to testify before a Congressional committee on the Klan's dealings. During the long hours of grueling questions, Forrest repeatedly had memory lapses and answered many questions with vague, public information that added nothing to the knowledge Congress already possessed. Undoubtedly he knew more than he let on but felt no obligation to share it with a government that he believed was stirring up trouble in his native South.

In keeping with his claim that his fight was not with Southern blacks, in August 1873, Forrest came to the defense of the black citizens of Trenton, Tennessee, after an incident involving two white men who came to a barbeque being hosted by the freedmen. The white men ate, then refused to pay, leading to a brawl between the two races. Sixteen blacks were subsequently arrested and jailed by the authorities, but a contingent of approximately seventy-five white men, some of them Klansmen, overtook the jail and lynched the black prisoners.

The fervor of this incident was felt all across the state, and meetings were held to determine a course of action. At an "indignation meeting" in Memphis, Forrest lambasted the white perpetrators as "white marauders who disgrace their race by this cowardly murder of negroes"[7] and volunteered to round up the men if the state would give him the authority. Forrest's offer was viewed with suspicion by some who thought his past sins were too big to overlook. Eventually he would find himself trapped between Northerners and blacks who distrusted him and Southern whites who were angered at him for defending the freedmen, a no-win situation where race relations were concerned.

Forrest and the Railroads

As a cavalry chieftain, Nathan Bedford Forrest was very familiar with the railroads. During the war, he and his men became masters at dismantling the tracks and wreaking havoc upon the Yankee attempts to supply their troops. Now with the war over, Forrest sought a reversal of his former ways, as he set out to rebuild the rail lines across the South.

In 1868, he bought an interest in the Cahaba, Marion, and Memphis Railroad and soon became president of the company under its new name: the Selma, Marion, and Memphis Railroad. As biographer Brian Steel Willis writes: "For the next five years of his life, Forrest devoted himself and his energies to this railroad. In the same personal style in which he had struggled to pull his family up from frontier semi-subsistence and with which he fought the war, Forrest supervised nearly every aspect of the construction, maintenance, and daily operation of this rail line."[8] Forrest immersed himself in the railroad work, spending time drumming up support, both political and financial, ordering supplies, and overseeing construction. Fundraising was always a problem and consequently one of the primary ways to raise money was to sell "subscriptions" to cities that would be served by the railroad. Many towns contributed in this way, but with the money came strings attached and suspicions aroused.

Forrest considered the railroad to be an extension of himself and felt his personal reputation suffered if the work suffered. On one occasion, he was notified that one of his contractors had failed to meet an obligation, and Forrest's legendary temper exploded. When he next encountered the contractor, a former Confederate colonel named A. K. Shepherd, he berated him for his incompetence and thoroughly offended Shepherd without giving him any opportunity to explain. So offended was the contractor that he promptly challenged Forrest to a dual, an offer Forrest hastily accepted. The rules and the date were set for the next day with pistols to be shot from ten paces. But, as sometimes happened, Forrest saw things in a different light when he had time to simmer down. As he tossed and turned the entire night, he came to the conclusion that his actions had been rash and wrong. Knowing that no one would ever question his courage, Forrest swallowed his pride, sought out Shepherd, and offered an apology. Shepherd gladly accepted and the issue was forgotten.

Forrest's temper almost landed him in trouble once again a short time later with another railroad colleague by the name of Minor Meriweather. A civil engineer who was given the job of certifying the completion of each section of the railroad, Meriweather determined that there was still work to be done. By certifying it complete, he would have triggered some of the pledge payments to be made to the railroad, payments that Forrest desperately needed to finish the job. Though various accounts came out about what happened, it is clear that Forrest threatened Meriweather, saying that if he made known his findings on the railroad, as he was scheduled to do the next day at a public hearing, Forrest would see to it he "didn't leave the room alive." The next day came, and as many anxious people gathered for the hearing, Meriweather went to the front of the room, set a pistol on the podium, and announced that if anyone had any problem with him they should make it known now since he did not want to be interrupted during his speech. All eyes were on Forrest, who directed his eyes to the ground, not saying a word. Once again his temper had subsided, and the meeting was completed without incident although bad blood remained between the two men.

Finances remained tight for the railroad project, and eventually it became clear that Forrest would never be able to raise the necessary funds for its completion. Numerous appeals to New England investors, Washington politicians, and Southerners failed to produce the needed capital. And though the board of directors issued a statement of confidence in his leadership, Forrest decided to step down as president of the railroad. Physically exhausted, financially strapped, and slightly bitter, Forrest tendered his resignation on July 1, 1874. He had poured all of himself into the production of the Selma, Marion, and Memphis Railroad, but all he had proved to be not enough.

Prior to the war, Forrest seemed to have the Midas touch. Everything he did resulted in huge profits. Now the opposite appeared to be true. His plantations had failed. His lumber business failed. His paving business failed. His insurance company failed. And now, his beloved railroad, which consumed several years of his life, had failed also. Forrest was becoming a broken man, both financially and spiritually.

It has been said that some people will not look up to God until they hit rock bottom, and certainly that would have been the case with the prideful Bedford Forrest. Life had become extremely tough for the former Confederate hero. Before the war he was wealthy and successful. During the war, he attained widespread fame as a hero in the South and villain in the North. But after the war, nothing seemed to go right. His fortune was gone. His fame was fleeting. His body was falling apart. And every business he tried, failed. But the trying circumstances of his life were being used by God for something far greater than worldly gain. Forrest did not understand it at the time, but God was using these failures as a hammer to obliterate his pride and draw him ever closer to the cross of Christ.

God's ways are infinite, and his grace can reach the vilest of sinners. For most of his life, Forrest had viewed God as a distant and secondary reality. Christianity was interesting to him, but he was content to be a sideline observer rather than a faithful partaker. That was about to change.

Chapter 9

That Devil Forrest Finds Redemption

"Therefore if anyone is in Christ, he is a new creature; the old things passed away; behold, new things have come." (2 Corinthians 5:17 NASB)

Nathan Bedford Forrest was quickly becoming a humble man. Like many men of his personality and temperament, the humbling process was not entirely voluntary, but life's circumstances and more importantly God's providence was leading him to a place of submission. Always the brash alpha-male, take-charge type, Bedford Forrest could now see his life's events slipping away from his normally firm grasp. Clearly, the Civil War marked a turning point in his life. Prior to the war, he had financially flourished in the world of slave trading and agriculture. Postwar, his last serious attempt at prosperity had come to an ignominious end. He was the president of a railroad company no more, and he would now go back to the agricultural world to make his living.

Life had come full circle for Bedford and Mary Ann Forrest. Their married life began in a log cabin in Hernando, Mississippi. Some thirty years later, they would move to a log cabin of the very same type on a rented plantation on President's Island, Tennessee. Having attempted to purchase a nice Memphis home from cotton merchant J. M. Farrington, Forrest was no longer able to make payments and had to move out—but not before spending a couple of weeks with the Farringtons, who were in the process of moving back in.

Mrs. Farrington's testimony gives us an interesting glimpse into the way Forrest was beginning to change. Farrington told of a kinder and gentler general who delighted in helping his wife around the house and took a strong interest in the Farringtons' children. As day gave way to evening, the aged and graying warrior would ease into a rocking chair. The Farringtons' young son would reach up and touch the general's beard and ask him to tell stories about the war. Forrest would gladly and dutifully oblige.[1] Though Bedford Forrest, even in his younger and wilder days, seems to have had a genuine love for children, an even more gracious and accommodating spirit can be seen at this point in his life. Partially, this can be attributed to the mellowing brought on by age, but we would be remiss if we did not take note of the spiritual changes coming to fruition in the general's life at this time.

Mary Ann Forrest had come from good Presbyterian stock, and it appears that she never wavered in her Christian commitment. A faithful member of the First Cumberland Presbyterian Church, also known as the Court Avenue Cumberland Presbyterian Church, in Memphis, she was now frequently accompanied to worship services by her aging husband.

To be sure, Bedford Forrest had always shown a reverence towards religion, but as his former regimental assistant and Methodist minister D. C. Kelley commented, Christianity was more of a "superstition"[2] to him than a real relationship with Christ. Chapel services and prayers were common in Forrest's army though perhaps they were more out of a desire to please a deity that would grant him success than a grateful heart of Christian love. When pressed by Christians about his own lack of a genuine relationship with Christ, Forrest would respond that he did not have time to become a Christian during the war, but maybe he would consider it afterwards. He had confessed on more than one occasion that he considered Christianity "a woman's religion." And yet it was "a woman's religion" that he gladly wanted the women and men of his life to accept and practice.

When the war was drawing to a close and Forrest was considering flight to Mexico, he wrote his son, William, exhorting him to care for his mother and to avoid the "sinful and wicked" ways in which his father had walked. When Fort Donelson was falling to U. S. Grant and the Union army, Forrest called Major Kelley to his side and implored him, "Parson! For God's sake pray! Nothing but God Almighty can save that fort!" Furthermore, he attributed his safety in battle to the prayers of his devout wife and mother. Like many in our world today, the Bedford Forrest of the Civil War was a man who wanted God's influence if it could benefit him in this temporal world yet refused to relinquish ultimate control of his life to the Lord's all-powerful care. He had wanted the rewards of Christianity without making any spiritual commitments of his own.

The pastor at Court Avenue Church was Rev. George Tucker Stainback, a native-born Virginian who had grown up in Alabama and Memphis. He had become a Christian in 1847 and subsequently entered the ministry. As pastor of the Court Avenue Church, he had garnered a reputation for deep piety and commitment to Christ. It was said that "he abhorred that which is evil, and he obeyed the injunction to cleave to that which is good."[3] Now Bedford Forrest, a man whose reputation in many circles was that of evil personified, was a regular attendee at his church.

God has a way of bringing Christian witnesses into someone's life when the Holy Spirit is leading them to salvation, and clearly this was happening in Bedford Forrest's life. Between Mary Ann's godly influence and example and Reverend Stainback's sermons, Forrest was absorbing much of the gospel message, but around this time in his life, another providential encounter would prove to be influential. Raleigh White had served as a colonel under Bedford Forrest during the war and the two had a chance encounter on the streets of Memphis. Forrest was both elated and shocked to see Colonel White, having heard that he was now living in another country. "So what have you been up to these days?" Forrest asked. White proceeded to tell the general of how his life had been dramatically changed. After the war, his wife had led him to faith in Christ and after dabbling in the business world, he had surrendered his life to the Christian ministry. Though not a Christian when he served with Forrest in the war, he was now a Southern Baptist pastor who had the honor of "preaching the gospel of the Son of God."

The effect this testimony had on Forrest must have been profound, given the fact that the two men's life stories were so similar. Both were non-Christians during the war. Both had godly wives influencing them. Both had escaped death numerous times on the battlefield. And both had failed in business after the war. Raleigh White had become a Christian. But what about Forrest?

Forrest was so moved by White's testimony that he did something quite out of character. He asked Raleigh White to pray for him. We do not know what exactly Forrest had in mind. Perhaps he simply wanted White to remember him in his private prayers, but the pastor went a step further than that. The two men walked off the street and entered a nearby bank lobby, where they both bowed down on their knees as White prayed for his former commander. Bedford Forrest was not a man who was bashful in public—many times he had killed men in public forums—but now he was showing an act of tremendous humility and gentleness as he kneeled with his minister friend.

Was transformation possible for Nathan Bedford Forrest? Though Raleigh White never had the pre-Christian reputation of ferocity that Forrest had, it had to have affected the general deeply to see the change exhibited in White's life. And it had to have stirred his heart to wonder if such change might come to him also. God's Spirit had used Raleigh White to plant another gospel seed that would soon come to fruition in the life of Bedford Forrest.

On November 14, 1875, Bedford was once again seated next to his wife at the Court Avenue Church as Reverend Stainback preached a message from Matthew 7, Jesus'

parable of the two builders. The words of Scripture struck
Forrest like a dagger in his heart:

> Therefore whosoever heareth these sayings of mine, and doeth
> them, I will liken him unto a wise man, which built his house
> upon a rock: And the rain descended, and the floods came,
> and the winds blew, and beat upon that house; and it fell not:
> for it was founded upon a rock. And every one that heareth
> these sayings of mine, and doeth them not, shall be likened
> unto a foolish man, which built his house upon the sand: And
> the rain descended, and the floods came, and the winds blew,
> and beat upon that house; and it fell: and great was the fall of
> it. (Matthew 7:24-27 KJV)

From the day of his birth Bedford had lived a life devoted
to building his "house." The hard-working son had dutifully
cared for his mother and siblings after his father's death.
Committed to escaping the squalor of eking out a meager
existence on the farm, he became a successful businessman,
amassing a fortune before the war. A hero of the Confederacy,
he recruited, trained, and led his cavalry troops into countless
battles, and his victories were impressive and legendary.
Successful in hand-to-hand combat he personally triumphed
over thirty men in battle. An early leader of the Ku Klux Klan
and a railroad executive, Bedford Forrest's life had been
devoted to building his prestige, power, and pocketbook.
But now he saw, ever so clearly, for the first time that it was
a kingdom of sand and would not carry him into eternity.
As life's failures began to accumulate for Forrest, he could
finally see that all his worldly success would never gain him
entrance into the eternal kingdom of heaven. For the first
time in his life, Nathan Bedford Forrest was a truly broken
man. And as the words flowed from the preacher's lips, the
tears swelled in Bedford's eyes.

As the church service ended on that November day in
1875, Bedford sought out Reverend Stainback. As Stainback
recounted years later: "Forrest suddenly leaned against

the wall and his eyes filled with tears. 'Sir, your sermon has removed the last prop from under me,' he said, 'I am the fool that built on the sand; I am a poor miserable sinner.'"[4] Finally, after fifty-four years of spiritual blindness, Nathan Bedford Forrest could see his condition and his desperate need for a savior.

What Reverend Stainback did next was both wise and fairly common in his day. Sermons can be very powerful and persuasive events in a person's life, but so can political speeches, music concerts, and theater productions. If the Spirit of God is genuinely bringing conversion to a sinner's heart, the effect will last beyond the initial moment of excitement.

Dr. Martyn Lloyd-Jones, the late pastor of Westminster Chapel in London, told of a night when he was preaching as a young pastor in Wales. He noticed that a man well known in town for his hard drinking and carousing was in attendance that night. And Lloyd-Jones could see the man sobbing throughout the message. As the man left the church that night, Lloyd-Jones shook his hand and wished him farewell, without pressing him for a Christian decision. The next night, Lloyd-Jones encountered the man in town and the two discussed the prior night's events:

> "You know, doctor, if you had asked me to stay behind last night I would have done so." "Well," I said, "I am asking you now, come with me now." "Oh no," he replied, "but if you had asked me last night I would have done so." "My dear friend," I said, "if what happened to you last night does not last for twenty-four hours I am not interested in it. If you are not as ready to come with me now as you were last night you have not got the right, the true thing. Whatever affected you last night was only temporary and passing, you still do not see your real need of Christ."[5]

Reverend Stainback did not want this to be a mere moment of excitement for Bedford Forrest. His sincere hope was that conversion was coming to his heart, and so he sent Forrest home with a spiritual assignment. He told him to read Psalm 51 for further guidance and then he would visit him the next day.

Psalm 51 is the quintessential Psalm to read regarding a repentant heart. Israel's King David penned the Psalm after being caught in what was to be his most vile transgression against God. David had an affair with Bathsheba, who was the wife of Uriah the Hittite, one of David's most loyal soldiers. After the affair, Bathsheba discovered she was pregnant with David's child, and in an effort to cover up his fatherhood, David ordered Uriah home from the front with orders to visit his wife. But Uriah's honor would not allow him to take part in the pleasures of home while his fellow soldiers waged war without him. So he disobeyed the king and camped with the king's servants at the palace. David then secretly ordered Uriah's commander to place him in the fiercest part of the battle and withdraw from him. This deep act of betrayal on David's part was meant to cover up his sin. But in fact, David learned that there is no escaping God, and shortly thereafter, David was confronted by the prophet Nathan (see 2 Samuel 12). David's heart, much like Bedford Forrest's, was crushed and as David contemplated his sin, he penned the words that centuries later would be read on that fall night in 1875 by the deeply distraught Forrest.

Have mercy upon me, O God, according to thy loving kindness: according unto the multitude of thy tender mercies blot out my transgressions. Wash me thoroughly from mine iniquity, and cleanse me from my sin. For I acknowledge my transgressions: and my sin is ever before me. Against thee, thee only, have I sinned, and done this evil in thy sight: that thou mightest be justified when thou speakest, and be clear when thou judgest. . . . Purge me with hyssop, and I shall be clean: wash me, and I shall be whiter than snow. Make me to hear joy and gladness; that the bones which thou hast broken may rejoice. Hide thy face from my sins, and blot out all mine iniquities. Create in me a clean heart, O God; and renew a right spirit within me. Cast me not away from thy presence; and take not thy holy spirit from me. Restore unto me the joy of thy salvation; and uphold me with thy free spirit. Then will I teach transgressors thy ways; and sinners shall be converted unto thee. . . . Deliver me from bloodguiltiness, O God, thou God of my salvation: and my tongue shall sing aloud of thy righteousness. The sacrifices of God are a broken spirit: a broken and a contrite heart, O God, thou wilt not despise. (Psalms 51:1-4; 7-14; 17 KJV)

The next evening, Stainback visited the Forrest home to further discuss the gospel and to pray with Bedford. Much like the moment with Raleigh White, both men bowed to their knees and prayed together. The exact words uttered are unknown to us, but the reality of a genuine conversion appears likely. After praying, Bedford said he was "satisfied." And that "all is right. I have put my trust in my Redeemer."[6]

For the first time in his life, Nathan Bedford Forrest completely submitted his life to Jesus Christ as Lord. He publicly professed his faith and became a member of the First Cumberland Presbyterian Church, which he had been attending with his wife. The apostle Paul wrote, "Therefore if anyone is in Christ, he is a new creature; the old things passed away; behold, new things have come" (2 Corinthians 5:17 NASB). Nathan Bedford Forrest the fighter, gambler, racist, and sinner famed for his bravado and ferocity in battle was a new creature in Christ. Humbled, broken, repentant, and at peace with his maker, Bedford Forrest, approaching the end of his earthly pilgrimage, began his new life in Christ.

Nathan Bedford Forrest's conversion brings to mind another well-known slave trader from Christian history. Like Forrest, John Newton was an obnoxious and violent man who had been born to a godly and pious mother. But Newton's mother died when he was seven years old, leaving him to the mercies of his seafaring father. In his early adulthood, Newton became a sailor in his own right but eventually deserted his captain and crew, only to be caught and publicly flogged for his infraction. He soon became the assistant to a violent slave trader in Sierra Leone before eventually making his way back to his native England, where he became the captain of his own slave ship. One night in 1748, while the ship was furiously tossed about on the high seas during a storm, John Newton cried out to the Lord for mercy. This began a transformation in his life that would lead him to become a faithful Christian, pastor, abolitionist, and in his spare time, hymn writer. Though he wrote hundreds of hymns, he is most well known for a very personal one that he wrote concerning his own past sins and eventual salvation. It is probably the most well-known hymn ever written.

> Amazing grace, how sweet the sound
> That saved a wretch like me!
> I once was lost, but now am found,
> Was blind, but now I see.
>
> Thro' many dangers, toils and snares,
> I have already come;
> 'Tis grace has brought me safe thus far,
> And grace will lead me home.

The words describe not only John Newton and Nathan Bedford Forrest, but also anyone who has walked in a life of sin only to be awakened by God's convicting spirit and graciously changed forever. Ultimately, it is that evidence of a changed life that validates the authenticity of a Christian conversion. In the gospel of Matthew, Jesus compares spiritual realities to fruit-bearing trees, saying, "You will know them by their fruits. Grapes are not gathered from thorn bushes nor figs from thistles, are they? So every good tree bears good fruit, but the bad tree bears bad fruit. A good tree cannot produce bad fruit, nor can a bad tree produce good fruit" (Matthew 7:16-18 NASB). Newton's life bore much fruit in ministerial service and public Christian influence.

Being sinners by nature, we are all prone to struggle with scores of individual deficits in our moral character. While

Bedford Forrest was no exception to this rule, there was one sin in particular that he is even today most remembered for: racism. As a slave owner and trader, he amassed a fortune from the sweat of the black man's brow and no doubt saw those who toiled under him as an inferior race. Such ignorant views are exposed today for the foolishness they clearly espouse, but this type of prejudicial thinking died hard in post-Civil War America. Though his degrading views towards blacks were very common in his day in both the North and South, these views were no less sinful because of their commonality. And clearly, Forrest acted upon his racial views beyond what many people even then would have been comfortable with. His involvement in the Ku Klux Klan only further sullied his reputation and spiritual state, even though he could have never known how far-reaching the Klan's diabolical influence would eventually be.

Clearly, Nathan Bedford Forrest was a racist, and any softening of his racial stand, especially in public, would have to be considered nearly miraculous. To speak out in defense of black people in the 1870s in Memphis would have been to invite ridicule upon himself. But speak out he did, and ridiculed he was. It was in the same general time frame of his Christian conversion in 1875 that Forrest was invited to attend a meeting of the Independent Order of Pole-Bearers Association, a civil rights group made up of black people in the Memphis area. One cannot help but try and imagine the unexpected sight of Nathan Bedford Forrest as the honored guest at a black civil rights function, but there he stood. And in his speech before this group, he clearly showed the fruit of his Christian repentance. The Nathan Bedford Forrest of 1865 was obviously not the same man who stood before the Pole-Bearers in 1875. His words on that day speak volumes about God's ability to change a man completely. And though many, to this day, malign Forrest for his past sins, his redemption is undoubtedly manifest in the words he spoke. After being presented a bouquet of flowers as a gift of reconciliation between the races by a young black lady named Lou Lewis, the aging and feeble general slowly arose and spoke, saying:

> Ladies and Gentlemen I accept the flowers as a memento of reconciliation between the white and colored races of the southern states. I accept it more particularly as it comes from a colored lady, for if there is any one on God's earth who loves the ladies I believe it is myself. (Immense applause and laughter.)
>
> I came here with the jeers of some white people, who think that I am doing wrong. I believe I can exert some influence, and do much to assist the people in strengthening fraternal relations, and shall do all in my power to elevate every man to depress none. (Applause.) I want to elevate you to take positions in law offices, in stores, on farms, and wherever you are capable of going. I have not said anything about politics today. I don't propose to say anything about politics. You have a right to elect whom you please; vote for the man you think best, and I think, when that is done, you and I are freemen. Do as you consider right and honest in electing men for office.
>
> I did not come here to make you a long speech, although invited to do so by you. I am not much of a speaker, and my business prevented me from preparing myself. I came to meet you as friends, and welcome you to the white people. I want you to come nearer to us. When I can serve you I will do so. We have but one flag, one country; let us stand together. We may differ in color, but not in sentiment.
>
> Many things have been said about me which are wrong, and which white and black persons here, who stood by me through the war, can contradict. Go to work, be industrious, live honestly and act truly, and when you are oppressed I'll come to your relief. I thank you, ladies and gentlemen, for this opportunity you have afforded me to be with you, and to assure you that I am with you in heart and in hand. (Prolonged applause.)[7]

One looks in vain to try and find any semblance of the former racist in Forrest's words. Yet what Bedford Forrest would do next was perhaps even more astounding. After his speech, the six-foot, two-inch Forrest leaned down and gently kissed Miss Lewis on the cheek, an act of acceptance and respect that was absolutely unheard-of for a white man to show towards a black woman in that day and age. Yes, this Nathan Bedford Forrest was not the same man who once sold slaves, gambled money, and killed Yankees. He was now a "new creature in Christ Jesus" and was beginning to show the fruit of it.

Chapter 10

Final Days

"By the sweat of your face you will eat bread, till you return to the ground, because from it you were taken; for you are dust, and to dust you shall return." (Genesis 3:19 NASB)

The Nathan Bedford Forrest of 1875 was a radically different person from the man of 1865, both spiritually and physically. Physically, time had taken a tremendous toll upon the warrior. By war's end, Forrest was a forty-four-year-old veteran with gray hair and an increasingly slow and limping gait. The ardors of battle, the long sleepless nights, the endless brawls, and the rigors of warfare had caused Forrest, as well as many veterans, to age well beyond his years. By Forrest's own account, he came back from the war "wrecked . . . completely used up—shot all to pieces, crippled up." The war took a physical toll on him from which he would never fully recover. His iron constitution was simply too depleted to work at the level he was accustomed to, but his determination and work ethic prevented him from slowing down. Eventually something would have to give, and it would be Forrest's body.

By the time of his conversion to Christianity in 1875, Forrest looked far older than his fifty-four years. His hair and beard were completely gray, and his once confident stride was now a slow, limping, and slightly slouching meander. He suffered from diabetes as well as "inflammation of the stomach" that left him with near constant pain and diarrhea. But through the breaking of his body, his spirit was renewed and he was at peace with his maker.

The first Sunday after his commitment to Christ, he publicly joined the membership of the Cumberland Presbyterian Church. At the end of the service, when the time came for those seeking membership to walk to the front, Forrest went without the slightest hesitation. Without awkwardness or shame, he claimed Christ as Lord and sought membership in the church. He was a changed man. And one can only imagine the jubilation his dear wife, Mary Ann, felt during this time. No doubt the years had been hard on her, but through it all she remained faithful to God and steadfast in her prayers for her wayward husband. She encouraged, cajoled, and calmed him, and when he would head out for a night of gambling, she would try to deter him and then tell him that she would be praying for him. This she did for decades.

Of his many vices, gambling was one of his greatest. After the war, when the Forrests were down to almost nothing, Bedford took ten dollars that Mary Ann had saved and gambled it at the poker table against her wishes. As he left the house he pleaded with her to pray for his success so that their financial situation would improve. Her response was that rather than gamble, they should live on less and eat half rations until things improved. Bedford went anyway and managed to win a large sum, but Mary Ann remained unimpressed by his immoral means of making the money.

This source of tension continued in their marriage, even to the period of his conversion. Forrest once again left the house one evening with plans to gamble his way out of a particular debt he could not pay. He told Mary Ann it was necessary in order to raise the needed funds; as usual she tried to dissuade him. She told him that while he gambled she would be on her knees with her Bible in hand praying for his spiritual conviction. This time it worked. As soon as Forrest won the sum he needed, he rose from the poker table and announced he was forever finished with the habit. The other players tried their best to change his mind, no doubt wanting to win back some of their losses, but Bedford was resolute. "My wife is sitting at home with a Bible on her knee. I told her I would quit as soon as I had enough money to pay my debt of honor. I am never going to gamble again."[1] With that a lifelong gambling addiction ended.

What brought about this sudden change in his habits? Mary Ann had pleaded with him for years to stop gambling. Why had she succeeded this time? The answer lies in something much deeper within Forrest. God was at work in his heart, and the Holy Spirit's conviction, coupled with his wife's steadfast testimony, was finally bearing fruit. It is unusual for a lifelong gambler to simply throw down his cards and quit without divine intervention. And spiritual convictions like these, which had long been evident in Mary Ann, were now also beginning to emerge in Bedford on many fronts.

The debt Forrest owed Mary Ann was incalculable. Through thick and thin she stayed by his side and was the very epitome of a gracious and godly wife. The Bible offers hope and instruction for women like Mary Ann, Christian women married to unbelieving husbands: "In the same way, you wives, be submissive to your own husbands so that even if any of them are disobedient to the word, they may be won without a word by the behavior of their wives, as they observe your chaste and respectful behavior" (1 Peter 3:1-2 NASB). Bedford spent the better part of his life observing and respecting her faith and love towards God and her husband. Now he, too, had embraced her Lord as his own.

Forrest's famous temper still gave him fits at times, but there was something different about him nonetheless. In a famous encounter with a Memphis tailor, Forrest showed signs of his old self. Arriving to pick up his suit of clothes, he discovered that it had been damaged by moths. True to his former nature, Forrest exploded with rage, verbally berating the tailor for such incompetence. The tailor was shocked at the temper and promised Forrest that it was an accident and that he would make full restitution. But Forrest pulled his pistol and leveled it at the stunned tailor. "Why General, you would not shoot me for such a trifle as that!" he said. "Yes! I'd shoot you like a rat!" Forrest snorted.[2]

Several factors gave rise to Forrest's reaction. For one, the former general physically felt horrible. He was in near constant pain and like most people, it had an effect on his personality. Financial stress was also a never-ending strain upon him during this time. Once a millionaire, he was now almost destitute, with bills piling up and no means to pay them. These extenuating circumstances do not excuse his behavior, but they do perhaps explain how a man could be so enraged at such a trivial matter.

But what about his newfound Christian faith? Just because a person becomes a Christian does not mean the battle with sin is over. Clearly there is a change that comes to a sinner's life when they are converted, but the "old" man dies hard. The same Bible that says, "Therefore if any man be in Christ, he is a new creature: old things are passed away; behold, all things are become new" (2 Corinthians 5:17 KJV) also teaches us, "If we say that we have no sin, we are deceiving ourselves and the truth is not in us" (1 John 1:8 NASB). The apostle Paul wrote of these struggles in his letter to the Galatians: "But I say, walk by the Spirit, and you will not carry out the desire of the flesh. For the flesh sets its desire against the Spirit, and the Spirit against the flesh; for these are in opposition to one another, so that you may not do the things that you please" (Galatians 5:16-17 NASB).

The deeper question when analyzing Christian faith is what does the person do after they have sinned? What is their response to the sin? Are they bothered by it? Are they spiritually convicted by it? Do they desire God's forgiveness? Do they seek to make things right with the offended party? The answer for a Christian, and for Forrest after this incident, was yes. The next day, Forrest returned to the tailor's shop with hat in hand. Broken and apologetic, he repentantly asked for forgiveness. The tailor was willing but still a little miffed. "Good gracious! General, can you do nothing with that temper of yours?" Frustrated with himself and his failure, Forrest shook his head and dejectedly responded, "I'll be damned if I can."[3]

This incident does not show us a perfect man, but it does show us a repentant one. A mere "baby in Christ," the fifty-four-year-old Forrest was still learning to live by the faith he had so recently embraced. While the perfect among us might cast stones at Forrest for his actions, any Christian who has struggled to overcome sin can relate to Forrest's frustration. The old ways die hard, for Forrest and for all of us, and, as with all people, the change would be gradual. Yet, the seeds of true Christianity were beginning to flourish, as evidenced by his contrition over the outburst.

In addition to being an aging warrior, Forrest was now also a grandfather. William had married and become the father of four children, who lived nearby. As Bedford and Mary Ann's only child to live to adulthood, William remained close, working as a railroad executive in Memphis while also helping his father run the farm. A familiar scene around Memphis in those days was Bedford coming to town to buy supplies. In the common work clothes of an everyday farmer, the unassuming man would slip in and out of town, oftentimes barely noticed. A visitor to Memphis would never have guessed that the weary old man at the general store was the famous General Forrest, renowned for his military prowess.

His rapidly failing health caused Forrest to frequently "take the waters" at Hurricane Springs, near Tullahoma, Tennessee. The warm, natural waters were thought by many to have health benefits, and by this point, Forrest was willing to try anything he could for relief. While there in 1876, Forrest received a visit from his former chief of staff, Charles Anderson. During the final days of the war, Anderson was the one who rode alone with Forrest as he contemplated whether or not to surrender. Anderson had seen Forrest at his most violent, so naturally he was shocked at what he now beheld. Anderson recounted:

> There was a mildness in his manner, a softness of expression, and a gentleness in his words that appeared to me strange and unnatural. At first I thought his bad health had brought about this change, but then I remembered that when sick or wounded he was the most restless and impatient man I ever saw. Soon I told him that there was something about him that I couldn't understand, that he didn't appear to me to be the same man I used to know so well. He was silent for a moment, then seemed to divine my trouble, and, halting suddenly, he took hold of the lapel of my coat and turned me squarely in front of him, and raising his right hand with that long index finger (his emphasizer) extended, he said, "Major, I am not the man you were with so long and knew so well. I hope I am a better man. I've joined the Church and am trying to live a Christian life. . . . Mary has prayed for me night and day for many years, and I feel now that through her prayers my life has been spared, and to them am I indebted for passing safely through so many dangers."[4]

Joseph Wheeler, the Confederate general whom Forrest butted heads with during the war, visited with Forrest in his final years and was also shocked by the change. His formerly powerful presence was now largely emaciated. His face was thin and pale, his movements slow and deliberate. But the most surprising aspect was his changed personality. Wheeler recounted: "Every line or suggestion of harshness had disappeared, and he seemed to possess in these last days the gentleness of expression, the voice and manner of a woman."[5] In nineteenth-century language, Wheeler was describing Forrest as a man who was now humble, meek, and Christlike in his attitude. The change must have seemed even more dramatic to Wheeler, who during the war had been the recipient of one of Forrest's legendary tirades, swearing he would never serve under him again. Now, Forrest was different. God had changed him.

Forrest late in life. Though in his mid-fifties, Forrest had aged well beyond his years. His fierce demeanor had been transformed into a meekness that stunned many of his former war comrades.

In one final act of humility, Forrest dropped lawsuits that he had filed against his former railroad in an attempt to regain some of his personal financial losses. John T. Morgan, his attorney and former war comrade, had been representing Forrest in the matters, but Forrest wrote to him and told him to drop all litigation, as recorded by one of his biographers.

> "I am broken in health and in spirit, and have not long to live.
> My life has been a battle from the start. It was a fight to achieve
> a livelihood for those dependent upon me in my younger days,
> and an independence for myself when I grew up to manhood,
> as well as in the terrible turmoil of the Civil War. I have seen
> too much of violence, and I want to close my days at peace
> with all the world, as I am now at peace with my Maker."
> He told General Morgan that he had for some time been
> attached to the Cumberland Presbyterian Church, and that he
> intended to live a peaceful and a better life for the remainder
> of his days. Although assured by his distinguished attorney
> that the suits were favorable to his interests, he persisted in
> their abandonment, saying he would not leave his only son a
> heritage of contention.[6]

Returning to Memphis, Bedford would spend his final days
alternating between his own home and the Memphis home
of his brother Jesse, which was closer to medical care. Once
a strapping two-hundred-pound mound of muscle, he now
weighed barely over one hundred pounds. He could not walk
without help and could scarcely keep down any food. Though
often in his final days he thought his recovery was eminent,
he soon realized, as did all, that his life was coming to an end.

Reverend Stainback paid Forrest a visit while he lay
suffering in his bed at home. He spoke with his pastor
about regrets he had over his past and even regrets for sins
committed after his conversion. Trusting in the promises
of God and Scripture, he felt the Lord had forgiven him
for his many failures. Forrest pointed his frail finger at his
heart and with a smile on his face said, "Just here I have an
indescribable peace. All is peace within. I want you to know
that between me and the face of my Heavenly Father, not a
cloud intervenes. I have put my trust in my Lord and Savior."[7]

Forrest spent his final days at the home of his brother Jesse.
There he took several visitors, including former Confederate

president Jefferson Davis, who was now living in Memphis. Forrest also received the company of Minor Meriweather, the old friend who had become an enemy in a railroad squabble. Sometime earlier, Meriweather and Forrest had patched things up, and Meriweather brought his son, Lee, to meet the dying general before it was too late. Forrest reached up and patted the boy's head, then looked up at Meriweather and said, "That's a fine boy, Colonel." Meriweather left the house with tears in his eyes, only to return by himself, volunteering to sit with Forrest during his death watch. And so it was Meriweather, a man who knew both sides of Forrest, a man who had experienced his friendship, his wrath, and by God's grace, his transformation, who heard Forrest's final words.

Near 7:00 P.M. on October 29, 1877, Forrest's final earthly thoughts turned to the one person who had supported him through it all. His thoughts were of the greatest Christian witness he had ever seen, the one who had prayed for him, struggled through life with him, calmed him, encouraged him, pleaded with him, and cared for him. Bedford opened his mouth for the final time and said, "Call my wife." Then he calmly closed his eyes, breathed his last breath of earthen air, and crossed over the threshold into a perfect world of infinite glory in the very presence of his Lord and Savior Jesus Christ. "That Devil Forrest" entered heaven.

Thousands of citizens, both white and black, thronged the streets of Memphis for Forrest's funeral. Politicians, friends, family, and ex-soldiers joined in the two-mile processional that led to his interment at Elmwood Cemetery. In death, just as in life, Forrest remained polarizing as the Southern newspapers mourned his passing and the Northern press declared good riddance. Regardless of the changes that came to his life, some refused to forgive him and were left to wallow in their own bitterness because of it.

His son, William, lived to be a successful businessman in the railroad industry that had financially crippled his father. He died in 1908 while attending a production of *The Clansman*,

Nathan Bedford Forrest III reached the rank of brigadier general in the United States Army. He was killed in action during World War II on June 13, 1943, near Kiel, Germany. (Courtesy of Tennessee State Library & Archives)

a play written about the Ku Klux Klan. Ironically, William was struck with a paralyzing stroke the very moment the actor portraying his father walked on stage. Mary Ann lived out her days in quiet fashion, helping William raise his children. She died in 1893 and was buried next to her famous husband.

While the sins of Nathan Bedford Forrest seem to dominate his legacy, his attributes are also well remembered.

His uncanny war instincts were second to none and have been studied by military students the world over. Though unfamiliar with the proper terminology, Forrest knew how to maneuver his men to take best advantage of the land and the enemy. And he knew how to fight. He famously said that he would "get there first with the most men" and time and time again he would do just that. Even when he had fewer men, he still usually won the day.

In 1892, an article was published by British field marshal Joseph Wolseley in which he praised Forrest for his phenomenal cavalry tactics and natural soldierly instincts. Having visited the Confederacy during the war, and having studied the war extensively afterward, Wolseley concluded that if Britain ever needed to fight for freedom they would be greatly helped by "as able a soldier as General Forrest."[8] Ironically, in the mid-twentieth century Britain would fight for its national identity against the German Nazism of Adolph Hitler, and Gen. Nathan Bedford Forrest would fight and die in defense of the British Crown. Brig. Gen. Nathan Bedford Forrest III, great-grandson of the Confederate chief, went down with his plane near Kiel, Germany, on June 13, 1943. His body washed ashore in September of the same year, and he was returned to America, where he is buried at Arlington National Cemetery. As he was the last male to be a direct descendant of Nathan Bedford Forrest, the Forrest name and soldierly legacy died with him. Yet, the Forrest legacy lives on.

Chapter 11

Forgiving Forrest

"Forgive us our sins, as we forgive those who sin against us."
(Matthew 6:12)

Perhaps the only thing more disturbing than an unrepentant sinner is the pompous rejection of one who does repent. All people are sinners, and all are called by God to forgive. Yet many hold grudges, even against those who are broken and contrite over their sin. They refuse to grant forgiveness and acceptance to those whom God has forgiven, and in so doing they set themselves up as authorities over the Almighty.

The New Testament gives a riveting account of a young woman who was caught in the act of adultery. While the woman was no doubt guilty and Jewish law called for her to be stoned to death, she was most likely used as an example to test Jesus. The Jewish Pharisees, an ultralegalistic sect of Judaism who hated Jesus, brought this woman before him to see what his reaction would be. If he said to stone her, then many of his followers might turn away from him, but if he said to let her go, then they would castigate him for disregarding the law. Without doubt the tension mounted as the crowd and the young woman waited to hear what Jesus would say. His words would change the world: "He that is without sin among you, let him first cast a stone at her" (John 8:7 KJV). The young woman was stunned. The crowd was stunned. The Pharisees were stunned. Thinking they had Jesus caught in the perfect theological trap, they were utterly mesmerized by his answer. The younger Pharisees looked to their older, wiser leaders and wondered what to do. The Bible tells us:

> And again he stooped down, and wrote on the ground. And they which heard it, being convicted by their own conscience, went out one by one, beginning at the eldest, even unto the last: and Jesus was left alone, and the woman standing in the midst. When Jesus had lifted up himself, and saw none but the woman, he said unto her, "Woman, where are thine accusers? Hath no man condemned thee?" She said, "No man, Lord." And Jesus said unto her, "Neither do I condemn thee: go, and sin no more."(John 8:8-11 KJV)

Jesus taught us to forgive. He clearly told us that he would forgive those who would humbly seek him through repentance and faith and calls his followers to do likewise. However, his followers sometimes struggle with this concept. The apostle Peter once asked Jesus how many times he had to forgive a repentant offender: "Then Peter came and said to Him, 'Lord, how often shall my brother sin against me and I forgive him? Up to seven times?' Jesus said to him, 'I do not say to you, up to seven times, but up to seventy times seven'" (Matthew 18:21-22 NASB). The point Jesus was making was that you can not put a number on forgiveness. If someone is burdened by their behavior and ask forgiveness, it is to be granted. Every time. All the time."Be kind to one another, tender-hearted, forgiving each other, just as God in Christ also has forgiven you" (Ephesians 4:32 NASB). Yet, even today, many refuse to grant such forgiveness to Nathan Bedford Forrest.

As Jesus taught, the only one with the right to withhold forgiveness from a repentant person is the one "without sin." The Bible clearly teaches that there was only one who ever lived without sin, Jesus himself, but modern people like to categorize their sins and in acts of self-justification usually consider their sins to be less heinous than someone else's. All who knew Forrest could testify to his many sins. He had some good qualities, but like all men, he was a sinner who struggled daily, and it could be argued that his sins affected more people than others' sins did. He was a slave trader who made his living by selling people for profit. He was a hot-tempered man who had more than his share of physical confrontations. He killed men, in times of both war and peace. He gambled, he cussed, and by anyone's definition, he was a racist. But all sins, including murder and racism, can be forgiven and covered by the grace of God through the blood of Jesus Christ.

Frequent attempts have been made over the years to have Forrest's name removed from public venues. Admirers build a statue to Forrest, and detractors, citing his history as a racist, cry for the statues to be torn down. Parks have been named for Forrest, as have schools and streets. While all Confederate leaders draw a certain amount of scorn from modern Americans, none come close to approaching the vitriol cast at Forrest.

Yet, Forrest could easily be held up by civil rights leaders as the very model of what they wish all racists would become. Far from castigating him for his sins, the civil rights community of today should praise him for the way he recanted and changed his views. In publicly encouraging the black people of his day to take up professional employment and seek public office, Forrest was showing himself to be far ahead of his time in terms of race relations. He took upon himself the scorn and ridicule that came from some white members of society when he vocally defended the black man's plight. One wonders if the civil rights community of today even knows the truth about what became of Nathan Bedford Forrest, for at the end of his life, Forrest was considered a liberal where racial matters were concerned. He was indeed the black man's friend, supporter, and even defender. When he died in 1877, thousands packed the streets of Memphis for his funeral, and many of those attendees were black. Some of them had forgiven him.

The apostle Paul wrote the Corinthian church, charging them to deal with an unrepentant sinner in their midst. A flagrant adulterer was flaunting his sin in the church while the Corinthian leaders did nothing. Paul commanded they confront him, and they did. He left the church and embraced his sin—for a season. Eventually he was broken and came back to the church, repentantly confessing his sin and seeking restoration. In their stubbornness they rejected him. They refused to forgive him, but Paul corrected their error. The purpose of dealing with the sin was to help the wayward man return to the path of righteousness. The discipline worked, but the Corinthians missed the point and refused to forgive him. Paul wrote them, "Sufficient for such a one is this punishment which was inflicted by the majority, so that on the contrary you should rather forgive and comfort him, otherwise such a one might be overwhelmed by excessive sorrow. Wherefore I urge you to reaffirm your love for him" (2 Corinthians 2:6-8 NASB). The sin may be heinous, but so is unforgiveness, especially towards a repentant man who seeks it.

History continues to malign the memory of Nathan Bedford Forrest, but Forrest found redemption in Jesus Christ, and in Forrest's story, we find hope for all sinners. In Forrest's story we see that no one is beyond the reach of God's grace. In Forrest's story we find hope that our loved ones who reject Christ might still have a change of heart in the end. In Forrest's story we see that God's grace truly is amazing. Jesus said, "Repent and believe the gospel" (Mark 1:15) and "All that the Father gives Me will come to Me, and the one who comes to Me I will certainly not cast out" (John 6:37 NASB). Forrest came to Christ. He came in humble, broken, repentant, obedient faith, and in so doing, he found redemption. Yes, through Christ, redemption is possible, even for a man like Nathan Bedford Forrest.

He was called many names in his life: peasant, pauper, farmer, racist, firebrand, killer, marauder, soldier, colonel, general, warrior, son, father, husband, brother. One Union general even gave him an unflattering name that would stick with him forever. Sherman derisively called him "that

Devil Forrest." But through the blood of Jesus, even "that Devil" from Tennessee can receive what no one can give but God alone. Indeed, the unthinkable happened, and by God's grace, we now know the story of the day when Nathan Bedford Forrest became a new creature in Christ. Therein lies the amazing, poignant, and glorious story of the Devil's redemption.

Amazing grace, how sweet the sound
That saved a wretch like me!
I once was lost, but now am found,
Was blind, but now I see.

Notes

Introduction
    1. *Memphis Bulletin,* May 18-19, 1865; Hurst, *Nathan Bedford Forrest,* 263.
    2. *War of the Rebellion: A Compilation of the Official Records of the Union and Confederate Armies,* ser. 1, vol. 39, pt. 2, 121 (hereafter cited as *O.R.*); Hurst, *Nathan Bedford Forrest,* 198.

Chapter 1
    1. Wyeth, *That Devil Forrest,* 10.
    2. Ibid., 16.
    3. "Concerning the Nathan Bedford Forrest Legend," *Tennessee Folklore Society Bulletin;* Ward, *River Run Red,* 16.

Chapter 2
    1. Davison and Foxx, *Nathan Bedford Forrest.*
    2. Arnold, *The History of Abraham Lincoln,* 124.
    3. Willis, *A Battle from the Start,* 41.

Chapter 3
    1. *Memphis Avalanche,* July 25, 1861; Hurst, *Nathan Bedford Forrest,* 73.
    2. Willis, *A Battle from the Start,* 47-48.
    3. Hurst, *Nathan Bedford Forrest,* 77-78.
    4. *O.R.,* ser. 1, vol. 7, pt. 1, 65; Willis, 53.
    5. White, 95.
    6. Blanton, "Forrest's Old Regiment," 41.
    8. Kelley, ed., *The Methodist Review,* 1012.
    9. Ibid.
    10. Ibid.
    11. Wyeth, *That Devil Forrest,* 47.
    12. Henry, *First with the Most,* 82.
    13. Hurst, *Nathan Bedford Forrest,* 95.
    14. Henry, *First with the Most,* 482.
    15. Davison and Foxx, *Nathan Bedford Forrest,* 98.
    16. Ibid., 101-2.
    17. Hurst, *Nathan Bedford Forrest,* 112.
    18. Foote, *The Civil War: A Narrative, Fredericksburg to Meridian,* 68.

Chapter 4

1. Wyeth, *That Devil Forrest,* 131-32.
2. Hale and Merritt, *A History of Tennessee,* 2280.
3. "Reverend James H. McNeilly: Chaplain, 49th Tennessee Infantry Regiment C.S.A.," available from Captain W. H. McCauley Camp 260 Dickson Co., Tenn. Web site, http://www.scvcamp260.org/mcneilly.html, accessed April 28, 2009.
4. McNeilly, "A Blessing for General Forrest," 279.
5. Wyeth, *That Devil Forrest,* 150.
6. Ibid., 163.
7. Willis, *A Battle from the Start,* 115.
8. Ibid., 119.
9. Ibid.
10. Leonidas Polk to his daughter, letter, November 15, 1863. Polk Papers, University of the South, quoted in Peter Cozzens, *This Terrible Sound: The Battle of Chickamauga* (Chicago: University of Illinois Press, 1992), 4.
11. William Gale to William Polk, letter, March 28, 1882, Polk Papers, University of the South, quoted in Cozzens, *This Terrible Sound,* 6.
12. Henry, *First with the Most,* 193.
13. Wyeth, *That Devil Forrest,* 242-43; Willis, *A Battle from the Start,* 146.
14. Wyeth, *That Devil Forrest,* 244.
15. Hurst, *Nathan Bedford Forrest,* 154.

Chapter 5

1. Anderson, "General Forrest Among Civilians," 212.
2. *O.R.,* ser. 1, vol. 32, pt. 3, 117; Willis, *A Battle from the Start,* 172.
3. Jordon and Pryor, *The Campaigns of General Nathan Bedford Forrest,* 422.
4. Ibid., 422-23.
5. *Detroit Free Press,* December 1, 1884, quoted in Ward, *River Run Red,* 141.
6. Ward, *River Run Red,* 142.
7. Davison and Foxx, *Nathan Bedford Forrest,* 228.
8. Winik, *April 1865,* 281.
9. Davison and Foxx, *Nathan Bedford Forrest,* 217.
10. Ibid., 11-12.
11. For several specific incidents, see Cicso, *War Crimes Against Southern Civilians.*
12. Davison and Foxx, *Nathan Bedford Forrest,* 241.
13. Hurst, *Nathan Bedford Forrest,* 177.
14. Willis, *A Battle from the Start,* 196.
15. *O.R.,* ser. 1, vol. 32, pt. 1, 609-10.

Chapter 6

1. Henry, *First with the Most,* 338.
2. Bolen, "Richard B. Alley and His Flag," 53.
3. Willis, *A Battle from the Start,* 313. Also quoted in Eckenrode, *Life of Nathan B. Forrest,* 169-70.
4. Henry, *First with the Most,* 437.

5. Willis, *A Battle from the Start,* 316.
6. Jordan and Pryor, *The Campaigns of General Nathan Bedford Forrest,* 681-82.

Chapter 7
1. Henry, *First with the Most,* 441.
2. Davison and Foxx, *Nathan Bedford Forrest,* 423.
3. Hurst, *Nathan Bedford Forrest,* 284.
4. Edmonds, *Facts and Falsehoods,* 240.
5. Ibid.

Chapter 8
1. Pickett, ed., *The American Heritage College Dictionary,* 545.
2. Horn, *Invisible Empire,* 428; Davison and Foxx, *Nathan Bedford Forrest,* 434.
3. Hurst, *Nathan Bedford Forrest,* 300.
4. Ibid., 302.
5. Willis, *A Battle from the Start,* 350.
6. Wade, *The Fiery Cross,* 59; Willis, *A Battle from the Start,* 358.
7. Hurst, *Nathan Bedford Forrest,* 361.
8. Willis, *A Battle from the Start,* 356.

Chapter 9
1. Hurst, *Nathan Bedford Forrest,* 359.
2. Willis, *A Battle from the Start,* 372.
3. "George Tucker Stainback: Cumberland Presbyterian Minister," available from Cumberland Presbyterian Denominational Headquarters Web site, http://www.cumberland.org/hfcpc/minister/StainbackGeorgeTucker.htm, accessed July 22, 2008.
4. *Memphis Appeal,* November 1, 1877; Hurst, *Nathan Bedford Forrest,* 370.
5. Lloyd-Jones, *Preaching & Preachers,* 275-76.
6. Hurst, *Nathan Bedford Forrest,* 370.
7. *Memphis Appeal,* July 6, 1875.

Chapter 10
1. Willis, *A Battle from the Start,* 372; Wilson, "Forrest, the Matchless Rider."
2. Hurst, *Nathan Bedford Forrest,* 369.
3. Willis, *A Battle from the Start,* 37.
4. Anderson, "My Last Meeting with Gen. Forrest," 387.
5. Wyeth, *That Devil Forrest,* 552.
6. Ibid.
7. Hurst, *Nathan Bedford Forrest,* 378; *Memphis Avalanche,* October 30, 1877; *Memphis Appeal,* November 1, 1877.
8. Henry, *As They Saw Forrest,* 47.

Selected Bibliography

Books

Arnold, Isaac Newton. *The History of Abraham Lincoln, and the Overthrow of Slavery.* New York: Clarke & Co., 1866.

Ashdown, Paul, and Edward Caudill. *The Myth of Nathan Bedford Forrest.* Lanham, MD: Rowman & Littlefield Publishers, 2005.

Bradley, Michael R. *Nathan Bedford Forrest's Escort and Staff.* Gretna, LA: Pelican Publishing Company, 2006.

Chapman, C. Stuart. *Shelby Foote: A Writer's Life.* Jackson: University Press of Mississippi, 2003.

Cisco, Walter Brian. *War Crimes Against Southern Civilians.* Gretna, LA: Pelican Publishing Company, 2007.

Cozzens, Peter. *This Terrible Sound: The Battle of Chickamauga.* Chicago: University of Illinois Press, 1992.

Cunningham, O. Edward. *Shiloh and the Western Campaign of 1862.* Edited by Gary D. Joiner and Timothy B. Smith. New York: Savas Beatie, 2007.

Daniel, Larry J. *Shiloh: The Battle That Changed the Civil War.* New York: Simon & Schuster, 1997.

Davison, Eddy W., and Daniel Foxx. *Nathan Bedford Forrest: In Search of the Enigma.* Gretna, LA: Pelican Publishing Company, 2007.

Eckenrode, Hamilton J. *Life of Nathan B. Forrest.* Richmond, VA: B.F. Johnson Publishing Co., 1918.

Edmonds, George. *Facts and Falsehoods Concerning the War on the South, 1861-1865.* Memphis: A.R. Taylor & Company, 1904.

Foote, Shelby. *The Civil War: A Narrative, Fort Sumter to Perryville.* 1959. Reprint, London: Vintage Books, 1986.

———. *The Civil War: A Narrative, Fredericksburg to Meridian.* 1963. Reprint, London, Vintage Books, 1986.

———. *The Civil War: A Narrative, Red River to Appomattox.* 1974. Reprint, London, Vintage Books, 1986.

Hale, William Thomas, and Dixon Lanier Merritt. *A History of Tennessee and Tennesseans: The Leaders and Representative Men in Commerce, Industry and Modern Activities.* Chicago: The Lewis Publishing Company, 1913.

Henry, Robert Selph. *As They Saw Forrest.* 1956. Reprint, Wilmington, NC: Broadfoot Publishing Co., 1987.

———. *First with the Most: Forrest.* New York: Mallard Press, 1991.

Hughes, Nathaniel Chairs Jr., Connie Walton Moretti, and James

Michael Browne. *Brigadier General Tyree H. Bell, C.S.A.: Forrest's Fighting Lieutenant.* Knoxville: University of Tennessee Press, 2004.

Horn, Stanley. *Invisible Empire: The Story of the Ku Klux Klan, 1866-1871.* Whitefish, MT: Kessinger Publishers, 2008.

Hurst, Jack. *Men of Fire: Grant, Forrest, and the Campaign That Decided the Civil War.* New York: Basic Books, 2008.

————. *Nathan Bedford Forrest: A Biography.* New York: Vintage Books, 1993.

Jordon, Thomas, and J. P. Pryor. *The Campaigns of General Nathan Bedford Forrest and of Forrest's Cavalry.* 1868. Reprint, New York: De Capo Press, 1996.

Kelley, William V., ed. *The Methodist Review.* 5th ser., vol. 15. New York: Eaton & Mains, 1899.

Lloyd-Jones, Martyn. *Preaching & Preachers.* Grand Rapids, MI: Zondervan Publishing, 1971.

Lytle, Andrew Nelson. *Bedford Forrest & His Critter Company.* 1931. Reprint, Nashville, TN: J.S. Sanders & Co., 2002.

Morton, John Watson. *The Artillery of Nathan Bedford Forrest's Cavalry.* Nashville, TN: Publishing House of the M. E. Church, South, Smith & Lamar, agents, 1909.

Pickett, Joseph P., ed. *The American Heritage College Dictionary.* 4th ed. Boston: Houghton Mifflin Company, 2002.

Wade, Wyn Craig. *The Fiery Cross: The Ku Klux Klan in America.* New York: Simon & Schuster, 1987.

Ward, Andrew. *River Run Red: The Fort Pillow Massacre in the American Civil War.* New York: Viking Press, 2005.

White, Henry Alexander. *Stonewall Jackson.* Philadelphia: G. W. Jacobs & Company, 1908.

Willis, Brian Steel. *A Battle from the Start: The Life of Nathan Bedford Forrest.* New York: HarperCollins, 1992.

Winik, Jay. *April 1865: The Month That Saved America.* New York: HarperCollins, 2001.

Wyeth, John A. *That Devil Forrest: Life of General Nathan Bedford Forrest.* New York: Harper & Brothers Publishing, 1959; Baton Rouge: Louisiana State University Press, 1989.

Articles

Anderson, Charles W. "General Forrest Among Civilians." *Confederate Veteran* 3 (July 1895).

————. "My Last Meeting with Gen. Forrest." *Confederate Veteran* 4 (November 1896).

————. "The True Story of Fort Pillow." *Confederate Veteran* 3 (November 1895).

Blanton, J. C. "Forrest's Old Regiment." *Confederate Veteran* 3 (February/ March 1895).

Bolen, David W. "Richard B. Alley and His Flag." *Confederate Veteran* 9 (February 1901).

Button, Charles W. "Early Engagements with Forrest." *Confederate Veteran* 5 (September 1897).

Clay, A. B. "On the Right at Chickamauga." *Confederate Veteran* 19 (July 1911).

"Concerning the Nathan Bedford Forrest Legend." *Tennessee Folklore Society Bulletin,* September 1938.

"Death of General Forrest's Wife." *Confederate Veteran* 1 (February 1893).

Faulkner, E. C. "The Last Time I Saw Forrest." *Confederate Veteran* 5 (February 1897).

Gray, H. T. "Forrest's First Cavalry Fight." *Confederate Veteran* 15 (March 1907).

Grief, J. V. "Forrest's Raid on Paducah." *Confederate Veteran* 5 (May 1897).

Hord, Henry Ewell. "Pursuit of Gen. Sturgiss." *Confederate Veteran* 13 (January 1905).

McNeilly, Rev. J. H. "A Blessing for General Forrest." *Confederate Veteran* 7 (October 1899).

Rhodes, Harry W. "Military Character of General Forrest." *Confederate Veteran* 4 (February 1896).

"Reunion of Forrest's Escort." *Confederate Veteran* 8 (July 1900).

Smith, Henry H. "Reminisces of Capt. Henry H. Smith." *Confederate Veteran* 8 (January 1900).

Steward, W. B. "Forrest's Raid into Memphis." *Confederate Veteran* 11 (November 1913).

Wilson, Florence. "Forrest, the Matchless Rider." *Nashville Banner,* July 7, 1935.

Newspapers
Memphis Appeal
Memphis Avalanche
Memphis Bulletin
Detroit Free Press

Government Records
U.S. War Department. *War of the Rebellion: A Compilation of the Official Records of the Union and Confederate Armies.* 128 vols. Washington, D.C., Government Printing Office, 1880-1900.

Index

_Dorn

Owens, William, 57

P
Paducah, Kentucky, 84
Parker's Crossroads, Battle of, 59-61, 68
Paul the Apostle, 15-17, 34, 67, 142, 150, 161-62
Peter the Apostle, 160
Pickering, Fort, 101
Pillow, Fort, 13, 113, 128-29
Pillow, Gideon, 53, 81
Planters Life Insurance Company, 124
Polk, Leonidas, 50, 74, 76, 82
Powell, Hannah, 116
President's Island, Tennessee, 135
Pulaski, Tennessee, 119, 121-22
Purdy, Tennessee, 82

R
Reed, Richard, 121
Rome, Georgia, 70-71
Rosecrans, William S., 76

S
Sacramento, Battle of, 86
Sacramento, Kentucky, 45-46, 57
Sand Mountain, Battle of, 70, 72
Sansom, Emma, 70-71
Selma, Alabama, 104
Selma, Marion, and Memphis Railroad, 132
Senter, DeWitt, 130
Seventh Tennessee Cavalry, 13
Seymour, Horatio, 128
Shaw, Wirt, 115
Shepherd, A. K., 132-33
Sherman, William T., 11-12, 15, 55, 68, 80, 97-101, 108, 162
Shiloh, Battle of, 54, 56, 77
Sierra Leone, 142
Sixth Tennessee Cavalry (U.S.A.), 81
Smith, Andrew, 99-101

Smith, William Sooy, 78, 80
Southern Life Insurance Company, 124
Stainback, George T., 137-40, 142, 154
Streight, Abel, 70-71
Sturgis, Samuel, 98-99
Sullivan, Jeremiah, 59

T
Tate, Thomas, 80
Taylor, Richard, 102
Tennessee River, 48
Terry, W. H., 47-48
Thompson's Station, Tennessee, 67
Tilgham, Lloyd, 48
Tippah County, Mississippi, 21
Trenton, Tennessee, 131
Tullahoma, Tennessee, 151
Tupelo, Mississippi, 52, 100
Twentieth Tennessee Infantry, 86

U
Uriah the Hittite (Old Testament), 141
U.S.S. *Carondelet*, 48
U.S.S. *New Era*, 87

V
Van Dorn, Earl, 67
Van Wick, S. M., 45
Vicksburg, Mississippi, 59

W
Washburn, Cadwallader, 98, 101-2
Wheeler, Joseph, 63-64, 76, 152
White, Josiah, 41
White, Raleigh, 137-38, 142
Willis, Brian Steel, 94, 132
Winik, Jay, 88
Wolseley, Joseph, 157
Woodbury, Tennessee, 57-58
Woodruff, John G., 94